NO STUDY
WITHOUT
STRUGGLE

NO STUDY
WITHOUT
STRUGGLE

CONFRONTING SETTLER
COLONIALISM IN
HIGHER EDUCATION

LEIGH PATEL

BEACON PRESS
BOSTON

BEACON PRESS
Boston, Massachusetts
www.beacon.org

Beacon Press books
are published under the auspices of
the Unitarian Universalist Association of Congregations.

24 23 22 21   8 7 6 5 4 3 2 1

This book is printed on acid-free paper that meets the uncoated paper
ANSI/NISO specifications for permanence as revised in 1992.

Text design and composition by Kim Arney

Library of Congress Cataloging-in-Publication Data

Name: Patel, Leigh, author.
Title: No study without struggle : confronting settler
colonialism in higher education / Leigh Patel.
Description: Boston : Beacon Press, 2021. | Includes
bibliographical references and index.
Identifiers: LCCN 2021003291 | ISBN 9780807050880 (hardcover) |
ISBN 9780807050910 (ebook)
Subjects: LCSH: Education, Higher—Social aspects—United States. |
Educational equalization—United States. | Social change—United States. |
Social justice and education—United States.
Classification: LCC LC191.94 .P375 2021 | DDC 306.43/2—dc23
LC record available at https://lccn.loc.gov/2021003291

This book is dedicated to all the study groups everywhere and to Thomas Nikundiwe, an education justice warrior of love.

CONTENTS

AUTHOR'S NOTE

When I was in elementary school, I learned about the thirteen colonies and how these were established by people from England seeking religious freedom. In sixth grade, my Hopkinton Middle School class took an hour-long bus ride to visit the Boston Tea Party Museum, where we listened to a short speech by a white man dressed in colonial-looking clothes. We then lined up to toss an empty cardboard box marked "TEA" that had been shellacked to resemble a wooden box. We tossed the "box" into the shallow water and then, using the attached slimy rope, pulled it back up for the next tween to simulate the fabled Tea Party rebellion.

At the time, I was more excited about the candy in the gift shop than any of the stories I was being told or invited to re-enact. And indeed, stories they were. Decades later, when I was invited to the Wôpanâak peoples' annual multiday Powwow event, not so far from that museum in Boston built to perpetuate myths, my eyes welled as parents, families, and teachers boldly celebrated the Native students who had graduated from elementary school, high school, and college. The accomplishments and the celebration of them defied centuries of cultural erasure and family separation through boarding schools, forced removal from homelands, and the US government's repeated violations of treaties. By then, I had learned a thing or two about colonialism, and, as the oft-quipped saying goes, once you know something, you cannot unknow it. This holds doubly true for colonial mythologies as well as the European invasion of Wôpanâak lands.

In actuality, another cliché, that history repeats itself, rings true. The practices of colonialism, along with the ubiquitous investment in them, continue today. But in other respects, the cliché falls short—reckoning with the various struggles against colonialism. This book highlights the intertwined nature of study and struggle. Whenever education, specifically higher education, has been made to reckon with its settler colonial structure, it has been largely through the struggles of those cast underneath the heel of oppression, fueled by their own formations to study.

There are many realms where settler colonialism operates, but formal schooling has been a main delivery system and key institution. From the Indian boarding schools in the early 1800s, whose avowed mission was "to kill savage to save the man,"[1] to contemporary curricula that both erase the ongoing histories of Native people and reinforce undeniably false and simplistic stories of the nation's formation, education has been crucial to the multifaceted project of settler colonialism. In fact, without schools teaching these falsehoods and perpetuating erasures, it would be much more difficult for colonialism's defenders to advance the theory of American success based on bootstrap individualism. Significantly, the very defenders who claim that this nation is meritocratic are often the beneficiaries of a centuries-long holocaust in which their ancestors seized Indian land and stole Black labor. The struggle to interrupt these narratives have been present throughout this history and in current contexts.

In November of 2019, the North Carolina State Board of Education rescinded its approval for an Indigenous-focused charter school designed by Drs. Rose Marie Lowry-Townsend, Brenda Dial Deese, Tiffany Locklear, and Denise Hunt—four women who are American Indians and have PhDs and wide experience in a variety of education settings and roles. They designed the school in the spirit of charter schools' original intent, which was to redress the failings of mainstream education. In this case, the purpose was to educate Lumbee and other students from an Indigenous-focused curriculum, providing them with dual proficiencies in state-mandated standards while maintaining and preserving Indigenous ways of knowing. The North Carolina Charter Schools Advisory Board rescinded the approval for the Old Main STREAM Academy twice, first on the basis of it not promoting unity, and then on the vague basis that "the school was not ready to open." One charter school review board member, Lindalyn Kakadelis, explained her rationale by using a secondhand summation of Quechua scholar Sandy Grande's book, *Red Pedagogy*. Kakadelis had not read the now-classic study of Indigenous ways of knowing and how they differ from Marxist analyses. Nonetheless, she assumed that the book greatly informed the charter school's application and countered the book: "I did not find one thing in the book that talked about the greatness of America. Now let me make it perfectly clear: America has sins. There are things I wish we had never done, slavery included. . . . Bad marks on our country. But we learned from them and we're changed and we're not what we used to be. I've got to say that everything I found was divisive instead of bringing unity."[2] Ironically, Grande's book, while a robust and oft-used text in Indigenous and decolonization studies, was not the basis of the charter school's curriculum.

Kakadelis's comments are objectionable because they are inaccurate. But more fundamentally, her comments and the moving line of approval, in essence, reveal what's behind the false narrative propping up this nation, which still delivers punishing material outcomes through settler power relations that seek to erase Indigeneity, contain Black peoples for profit, and exploit migrant labor for the purpose of hypermasculine global dominance. Many have spoken Kakadelis's message of unity over division, but it is too often thrown in the laps of those who must give up significant parts of themselves to be part of that unity. In the case of the Old Main STREAM Academy in North Carolina—or more accurately, in Lumbee territory—for the Lumbee children, their lived realities cannot exist side by side with colonialist narratives without exposing them as lies. These children might also be expected to assimilate into a US meritocracy that still holds little but violence and erasure for Native peoples. Put more simply, Kakadelis's claim that "we" have learned from the occasional mistakes, even sins, of the past is patently wrong. On the contrary, her dismissal of Grande's book shows how, without even reading it, the book's existence presented a threat to settler narratives of national advancement.

I draw attention to this example because it pulls into focus many of the intersections covered in this book: the ongoing structure and grip of settler colonialism, the myriad ways in which people have resisted it, and the central place of study in the struggle for a more just society. To make this point, I could have discussed the backlash to ethnic studies in Tucson, Arizona, the federal closing of Black Saturday schools founded by the Black Panther Party, the 1921 burning of the largely Black-owned and -led district of Greenwood in Tulsa, Oklahoma, or the mass hanging of Dakota men ordered by Abraham Lincoln in 1862 to make this point. I chose a recent example to underscore the fact that study and sovereignty have always had a tenuous, if not exploitive, power relation in formal education. I wrote about this example at a time when this nation is tested by many stressors: a global pandemic in which this nation has steadily led in rates of infection and death, unemployment levels not seen since the Great Depression, and a persistent flow of uprisings against anti-Black racism that continued even when much of the nation sought to shelter-in-place from the pandemic. The nation has on its hands two pandemics, the novel coronavirus and a pandemic of anti-Black racism. Yet, it also faces a familiar plight: reconciling word and deed. The nation still upholds itself as the land of opportunity, where liberty, justice, and pursuit of happiness are on offer for all. Yet, during 2020 alone, the nation watched as thousands protested the robbing of Black life at the hands of militarized law enforcement and white men who had deputized themselves. Although the nation's words assert its excellence and talent, its deeds, devaluing most peoples' lives and favoring individualism over collective wellness, were on full display, with Donald Trump, a lifelong explicit racist and misogynist, for years tweeting lies from the highest office in the land and refusing to concede electoral defeat despite clear evidence that he lost. These are not aberrations; they are but a few of the thousands of data points from a nation that has a beautiful declaration of independence, written and signed largely by white men who enslaved people.

As a key institution in this society, education has also been stretched between its avowed duty to educate for democracy and its practices of creating obstacles in the form of high-stakes assessments, the closing of schools in Black and brown neighborhoods, and corporate models of higher education governance. The times we live in are precarious; however, they are far from unprecedented. History and unfolding contemporary realities have much to teach us about the intertwined practices of oppression and the resistance and solidarity of many.

In this book, I demonstrate how the ability to study has involved struggle by virtue of the nation's origins and ongoing structure of settler colonialism. I use historical records, oral histories from some of the land's most experienced activists for educational access, and examples of contemporary power relations to illuminate the distinct yet deeply connected tactics of settler colonialism.

Study and struggle are enacted together in many ways. For example, protests, marches, and sit-ins are forms of public pedagogy. In essence, they are actions that are meant to teach the public and shift its ideas about racism, poverty, labor exploitation, and other issues. This is a form of pedagogy, of teaching and learning; it is not carried out for the sake of awarding grades but rather, in the interest of shifting mindsets and material realities. These forms of public pedagogy sometimes emerge from and are intricately tied to internal political education. "Internal," in this sense, means it occurs in an organization or group, not within one person's education. Almost always, before a sit-in happens, groups of people have gathered, thought together, often read together, made or engaged in the appreciation and creation of art that reaches beyond what theories offer, and mutually taught each other to politically analyze their and others' lived realities. Other times, such as in the protests in the summer of 2020 against the legal and extralegal killings of Black people, uprisings and rebellions give way to a renewed education about racism, its origins, and its ongoing hold in law enforcement, medicine, and education, to name a few core institutions that act as delivery systems for oppression. In short, struggle has always involved study, and study inevitably leads to demand and struggle. As la paperson explains in their book, *A Third University Is Possible*, as soon as colonization began, so did practices of decolonization. Rather than existing in a binary relation to one another, study and struggle defy categorization as anything other than a vibrant trying, failing, learning joint entity. In other words, the experience of being alive.

I bring to this book my experience as a professor, a university administrator, a person involved in grassroots organizing for education for liberation, and the discipline of a writer who was informed by the teachings of people like the late journalist Gwen Ifill. All these influences make this book, I hope, difficult to categorize. My background as a journalist has disciplined me to get the facts right and cut the idea close to the bone. Historical research demands starting the story in the right place, and scratching at the surface of facile renderings to learn what was added to and erased from historical accounts. Learning about political organizing as an adult in education liberation efforts taught me, viscerally, that social movements and the public good belong to the commons, a subtle yet powerful distinction. Public entities, such as parks and schools, may seem open to the public, but often are owned and surveilled by private entities or run through corporatist justifications of lifting up achievement and casting aside those who are not in the #1, A-plus club. Corporate-like charter schools are a poignant example of schools being available, purportedly, for the public good but not belonging and being answerable to the commons.[3]

Working in academia has provided me with both opportunities and consequences for teaching about the history and ongoing power structures of settler colonialism. I have been able to find windows, side streets, and passages for rigorous reading and work, and I am always grateful to be in study groups with my compatriots in learning. Classrooms, mentoring, collaborative work: some of the richest writings and collectives for justice have come about, in part, through formal education, in the created spaces of collective learning that can exist in classrooms. More often, they come about by being sparked in those spaces but moving beyond them quickly.

I hope this book provides you with a grounding in the relationship between study and struggle, between higher education and settler colonialism. I hope it reminds you that there is a big difference between being a high-achieving student and being a learning, failing, striving, and slightly skeptical human being. I hope it reminds you of the interconnectedness of all living beings and that property is itself a violent concept. Finally, as Dr. Mariame Kaba consistently reminds her many social media followers and those who work with her for prison abolition, hope is a discipline. It is to be practiced, renewed, and maintained.

CHAPTER ONE

STUDY AND STRUGGLE

"Campus Protests Are Spreading Like Wildfire"
       —*MOTHER JONES*, November 19, 2015[1]

"Do US Colleges Have a Race Problem?"
       —CNN, November 10, 2015[2]

"One of the paradoxes of education was that precisely at the point when you begin to develop a conscience, you must find yourself at war with your society."
       —JAMES BALDWIN, "A Talk to Teachers," 1963[3]

In 2016, historian Robin D. G. Kelley published an essay in a series in the *Boston Review* entitled "Black Study, Black Struggle."[4] In this precise yet concise piece, Kelley explains how the uprisings against racism on college campuses are best understood as part of an ongoing relationship between cries for freedom in the streets and those on campuses. Kelley references several rebellions that occurred before the 2015 protests in Ferguson, Missouri, decrying eighteen-year-old Michael Brown's death at the hands of a white police officer. Among them, for example, is the Watts Rebellion, a six-day uprising in Los Angeles in 1965 that occurred after police officers pulled over a formerly incarcerated Black man, Marquette Frye, and proceeded to beat him and members of his family. Within hours, hundreds of Black citizens were in the area, protesting the physical blows that the white police officers dealt to Frye and family members.

"It all started with a traffic stop," reads the opening sentence of a 2020 *Los Angeles Times* story. In actuality, the uprising's roots were planted long before Frye was stopped by the police.[5] As reporter James Queally goes on to explain, the Watts Rebellion is intricately tied to the Great Migration of Black Americans out of the Jim Crow South and into other US regions. The Black population in Los Angeles grew from 63,000 in 1940 to 753,000 in 1970, largely concentrated in the south-central part of the county. This area had poorly resourced schools and severely limited public transportation, which social geographer and scholar activist Ruth Wilson Gilmore cites as both a form of containment and often a precursor to uprisings. Gilmore explains that a decade before the Frye incident, in which yet another Black person's right to exist was immediately put into question, the Watts schools had opted for more centralized control, and that led to more suspensions of Black students from under-resourced elementary and secondary schools.

The Watts Rebellion was long-simmering and sparked by a traffic stop that turned into an all-too-familiar scene of white police violence on Black peoples. The unrest and rebellion shook the city, specifically the city's white neighborhoods and their image of sun, beaches, and fame—for some. Although hundreds of protesters were active for six days, the deployment of fourteen thousand California National Guard troops says more about the white fear of this Black uprising. The campus protests of the late 1960s are often cited as an important time and space for mobilization and a call for social transformation, but the analysis of the rebellion fails to consider what took place before. Kelley's discussion of the Watts Rebellion makes explicit not only that the relationship between public protests and campus protests has been close, but that the uprisings in the streets have almost always preceded campus uprisings. Additionally, he reminds readers that uprisings themselves are rooted in histories of enclosure, restriction, and poverty, all social conditions that were and continue to be animated by anti-Black racism.

Kelley's essay, followed by several stunning responses from public intellectuals including Barbara Ransby and Keeanga-Yamahtta Taylor, highlights the fact that there is a long precedence of Black peoples' struggle to study and techniques that Black students have used within universities to rework how resources and gatherings are formed. "Struggle," in Kelley's essay and in this book, does not mean suffering and pain but people's rigorous engagement with each other and differing ideas of freedom. Building on this understanding of struggle, where no experience is assumed to be shared or universal, Kelley also provides several cautions against overestimating the proportion of Black students participating in campus protests, as they make up only a fraction of the total enrollment of Black students. But the numbers are not as important as their organizing and their demands. He speaks frankly to the fissures within the student protests and their demands in the late 2010s, including that related to relief from racist harm inflicted by colleges steeped in white supremacy. Kelley also expresses his worry that a focus on trauma will collapse a systemic analysis of the conditions that create that pain. He urges student activists to discern between reform and revolution, a fundamental question that shapes almost every social movement's demands and potential impact.

Kelley's essay, as well as the responses to it, including Black Studies professor Barbara Ransby's points about stealing back from universities that have engaged in extraction from Black, migrant, and Indigenous communities and lands, all bring to bear fundamental questions about the struggle to study, live, and thrive within fundamentally oppressive institutions and societies. Kelley writes, "Black studies was conceived not just outside the university but in *opposition* to a Eurocentric university culture with ties to corporate and military power." He states clearly that he does not see the university as an engine for social change, nor a place capable of loving the students that it actively dehumanizes through its research, its Eurocentric pedagogies, and its investments in prison systems and planet-plundering industries. And yet, Kelley and many authors, including me, have much still to say about and to higher education. Moreover, professionals in higher education are listening to and learning alongside students, which includes tussling over demands such as the call for safe spaces. This call has been expressed in many ways, including the demand that students be free from reading about oppression from the perspective of the conqueror, and that colleges' statues and building names stop honoring men who enslaved Black peoples. Being omitted completely from curricula creates a distinct form of harm for students, including white students, as they become more entrenched in the ideology of white supremacy, without being taught the harm that white supremacy has done. For example, K–12 students still learn that Christopher Columbus "discovered" America, and that myth is furthered in higher education. The struggles to learn by marginalized students is itself a form of love, not romantic love but the love of learning and its inextricable relationship with life itself.

This is a book about higher education, but it is also fundamentally about the struggle to be able to study and the important place study has had in social movements that have fought for access to learning in higher education and education for social transformation. Fortunately, there is a long history of the intertwined nature of study and struggle to inform contemporary protests and uprisings, all of which included a love for a better society. This book is about the long-standing and intertwined nature of struggle and study.

There have been many books and articles about specific social movements, and books and articles about higher education. In this book, I suggest that naming the problem of racism in higher education is necessary but insufficient. Settler colonialism, an ongoing structure of many nations, including the United States, offers a more comprehensive framework explaining why marginalized populations experience distinct yet deeply connected forms of harm and barriers to higher education.

The existence of racism, although a durable global phenomenon, does not alone provide a robust enough explanation for the practices and habits of thought that bolster many of higher education's problems. These problems include rising tuitions; soaring student loan debt, more so for Black students; an imbalanced Eurocentric curriculum; and the shrinking number of faculty jobs, in favor of low-paid adjunct faculty. At the same time, higher education faces a public relations crisis. The system of white supremacy has resulted in higher ed being historically and persistently white. The ongoing erasure of Indigenous peoples through Eurocentric curricula and the lack of accurate education about Indigenous lands upon which universities sit upon results in a miseducation and mixed messages from campuses that celebrate diversity in their brochures and websites, but in reality function as sites of whiteness.

Enslaved peoples literally built the nation's most elite institutions. In contemporary contexts, the majority of funding for public K–12 school districts comes from local property taxes. This means that the zip code into which children are born and their racially segregated neighborhoods determine their educational opportunities. All too often, students descended from enslaved and erased ancestors attend resource-deprived elementary and high schools and are likely to grow up in families that are purposefully cordoned off from generational wealth. These young people and their families are more likely to experience intermittent employment opportunities and be hired for low-paid hourly work. Strained economic conditions rob students of time to learn not just curricula, but also build social networks that more affluent young people experience through schooling, out-of-school activities, and family connections to those in power. Young people juggling work and their family's needs to make it from one paycheck to the next face much larger hurdles and obstacles than their counterparts in well-funded schools and wealthier neighborhoods with greater access to fresh food, public parks, and well-funded schools.

As a result of these divides of white supremacist policy and its cultural practices, Black people, Indigenous people, and people of color (BIPOC) must contend with generational wealth scarcity. For Black students, their barriers to generational wealth have been enshrined into law and code since 1619. Latinx students often are saddled with rote instruction, because rather than being seen as emergent bilingual people, they are treated as behind monolingual US-born students. Native students must contend with reading history texts that speak about them as belonging to a people mistreated and now simply gone. Transgender students encounter transphobia from people and institutions when, for example, the custom of binary gender–defined bathrooms on campus communicates to them that their basic humanity is not recognized. Barriers to higher education take many forms, and although different populations experience different forms of discrimination, they are connected through the larger structure of settler colonialism.

The list of the ways that differently minoritized populations have been pushed to the margins, blocked from higher education, or provided inadequate education is long and varied.[6] Just as long and varied, though, is the set of specific knowledge systems that many marginalized young people learn in and from their caregivers. Rarely, though, is the considerable wisdom a young person has acquired in their largely working-class or working-poor neighborhood reflected in any of the curricula or assessments that formal education employs.

Racism, specifically anti-Black racism, is essential to understanding many of the complex problems in the country and its higher education system; however, it is not the definitive analytical tool. In fact, no one analytic can adequately and consistently encompass the varied and shifting forms of oppression, so the challenge is to use lenses that best fit our questions, frustrations, and needs without insisting that one sole view can account for all dynamics of power in society. As Rachel Herzing, executive director of the Center for Political Education and cofounder of Critical Resistance, a long-standing grassroots organization dedicated to abolishing the prison industrial complex, reminds her readers, political education necessarily requires that we never stop learning: "The time when you think you've got it all figured out is probably the time you need to push yourself to learn even more."[7]

Upon learning that there is no end point where one has figured out all of oppression and how to dismantle it, we are also reminded of the functions of various analytic tools and how they prompt us to ask different, perhaps better questions. Settler colonialism allows for and demands a broader understanding of how racism, property accumulation, erasure, and gender binaries are used to maintain extractive power dynamics in education, in part because of the place that education holds in the general imaginary and the specific geographies in which formal education takes place.

We speak of education in terms of its potential to be the great equalizer. An example that I have revisited several times is then president Obama's introduction of Sonia Sotomayor as his nominee for the Supreme Court. In his remarks, Obama spoke of her consistent efforts to learn at every opportunity and the sacrifices her Puerto Rican family, particularly her mother, made to send her to a private local school in their South Bronx neighborhood, Cardinal Spellman Elementary. As narrated by President Obama, Sotomayor's family made these choices out of the belief that in America, with a good education, all things are possible.[8] It is, simply put, a well-worn narrative of success through pulling one's self by their own bootstraps, grit, and determination. In Sotomayor's 2013 autobiography, written just before she took her place as a Supreme Court justice, she invites us to go further into the story of her childhood, the details of her family's dynamics, and grapples with the fact that for a family unit like hers, there are no guarantees of the American Dream opening up unfettered opportunities. She elegantly describes the various contexts that shaped how she came to understand herself and society. She shares about some of the complexities in her parents' relationship, including her father's alcoholism, her mother's frustrations, and the verbal altercations that resulted in her mother becoming her primary caregiver and working several jobs to send Sotomayor to a private school that she assumed would provide her daughter with a better education. In her memoir, Sotomayor explains the chasm between her mother's perceptions and the hyper-disciplined nature of her Catholic elementary school in the South Bronx, the one Obama mentioned in his remarks:

> I often stewed with righteous anger over physical punishments—my own or others' . . . . In time I would find my own satisfaction in the classroom. My first years there, however, I met with little warmth. In part, it was that the nuns were critical of working mothers, and their disapproval was felt by latchkey kids. The irony of course was that my mother wouldn't have been working such long hours if not to pay for that education she believed was the key to any aspirations for a better life.[9]

Although not borne out by facts and statistics, this widely held narrative of education being the great equalizer connects with another widely believed narrative about the nation being a melting pot built by immigrants. In President John F. Kennedy's book *A Nation of*

Immigrants, he furthered that narrative, which he advanced through-out his career, explaining that this nation's responsibility should be to welcome immigrants so they can pave their way to social mobility, or as it is more commonly known, the American Dream.[10] In the open-ing pages of this book, written in 1958 but published posthumously in 1964, the widely loved Kennedy lifts up the national narrative of immigrants building the nation while, in keeping with the colonizing message, rapidly discounting and largely erasing the existence the hundreds of Native tribes and nations preceding the arrival of the first European ship holding enslaved Black people in 1619:

> Every American who ever lived, with the exception of one group, was either an immigrant himself or a descendant of immigrants. The exception? Will Rogers, part Cherokee Indian, said his ancestors were at the dock to meet the *Mayflower*.[11]

Kennedy's qualifier of Will Rogers as part Cherokee works to erase the ways that Native peoples preceded Europeans. He con-tinues with this erasure of Native peoples' origin stories, citing un-named anthropologists to make the following claim:

> And some anthropologists believe that the Indians themselves were immigrants from another continent who displaced the original Americans—the aborigines.[12]

While there is no doubt that immigrants have played an import-ant role in the rise of the United States as a world power, Kennedy's words are both wrong and, more worrisome, widely perpetuated through school curricula and racist mascots that depict Native peoples as warrior men of the past. The belief that this is a nation built by immigrants does several things at once: It erases origin sto-ries and relationships to land that are fundamental to Indigenous knowledge systems. It lionizes immigrants while erasing the shifting forms of xenophobia directed at migrants throughout the history of the United States. Lastly, it skips across important junctures of solidarity, including Irish immigrants' initial solidarity with Black peoples out of a recognition of being cast as the scourge of a society.

The role of migrants to the United States is far more complicated, riddled with racist nationalism, violence, and opportunism wielded by those in power. This complicated reality also erodes the national mythology and symbolism that politicians of both political parties consistently advance, gesturing to symbols of freedom and liberty, such as the Statue of Liberty and the nation's Declaration of Independence, as evidence of equality. The alluring narrative that this is a nation that opens its arms to immigrants has quite simply never been the case. We have been taught lies and we have learned to love those lies, as poet-activist Darnell Moore puts it in his memoir, *No Ashes in the Fire*.[13] Moore and, before him, bell hooks, have talked about this kind of harmful love, as something so superficial that it barely qualifies as love, incapable of reckoning with the truth.

The narratives of education as the great equalizer and America as a melting pot gloss over the reality that the nation came to be a world power by building its wealth through stolen labor on stolen land. The project of settler colonialism, an ongoing power structure, manifests itself, in part, through racist capitalism, but it has many structural components that are not limited to racism. It put into motion policies and cultural practices that removed and even decimated Indigenous populations, and imported enslaved peoples to literally till prosperity from that stolen land. It has used ideas of gender binaries and the ideal heteronormative nuclear family as another way to create "others," unfit for essential rights that are always revocable by those whose rights are unshakeable. Out of this unseemly mix, much of the nation's institutions were created, including its most celebrated private and public universities.

Despite the wide availability of facts about income, opportunity, and obstacles, these narratives about education—of it evening out the social playing field and offering someone the chance to pull themselves up by their bootstraps—persist with undeniably real material impacts. For example, home ownership for Black millennials lags far behind that of their white counterparts, by as much 24 percent.[14] Alanna McCargo, vice president for housing finance policy at the Urban Institute, a nonprofit agency that keeps tabs on the rates of home ownership, underscores the point that Black students carry more student debt than their white and Latinx counterparts. Without generational wealth, debt accrues, which cycles back to keep home ownership out of reach. She summarized the generational impact of Black families' lack of access to housing security: "Not achieving higher Black homeownership rates has thwarted economic mobility and stifled generations of wealth building. The persistent racial homeownership gap is leaving millions of Black families behind, and without access to a key asset and wealth building tool that has intergenerational implications for overall financial well-being."[15]

Additionally, Black students are more likely to default on student loan debt, because of that lack of generational wealth and job opportunities, let alone equitable pay practices. In other words, white young adults benefit from de jure and de facto practices that have allowed white families to accrue wealth carried across generations, while Black, Indigenous, and migrant families more typically live paycheck to paycheck.

Despite the increasingly diverse ethnic makeup of the country, enrollment rates at community and four-year colleges continue to be disproportionately higher for white people, particularly compared with the enrollment rates of growing Latinx communities. Roughly 60 percent of Latinx people in the United States are under thirty-five, prime college-attending years, but of that population, there was an increase in college enrollment of approximately 20 percent in 2018.

White students made up 43 percent of students enrolled in college programs in 2018.[16] Moreover, as college loan debt rises, BIPOC carry more debt and are less likely to be employed and therefore have incomes that can chip away at that debt.[17]

The Fair Housing Act of 1968 was meant to eradicate race-based housing and loan qualifications riddled by redlining, racism, and bigotry.[18] In 2013, a study by sociologists Brandon Jackson and John Reynolds uncovered a startling statistic: Black college graduates were forty-seven times as likely to default on college loans than white counterparts.[19] Between 2005 and 2015, the homeownership rate among white young adults was 38.5 percent, compared with 28.8 percent for Hispanics, and 14.5 percent for African Americans. With home ownership intricately connected to racist housing policies that have led to racially segregated neighborhoods and uneven property taxes that drive the inequity in K–12 education, it should come as no surprise that for centuries, Black people have been systematically blocked access to the so-called American dream: upward social mobility through higher education.

There are basically two possible explanations for these statistic trends: either nonwhite populations are not as skilled or motivated to find employment, or there are structural barriers that create obstacles to financial security for graduates of color and their families. Statistics help here also. Almost without fail, each year, the unemployment rate for Black peoples in the US doubles that of white unemployment. Additionally, study after study has shown that in job application situations, people with "ethnic-sounding names" are not called back after a phone inquiry. Although there have been some important milestones showing progress for unemployed and underemployed Black Americans, this does not account for millions of undocumented Black workers or Black youth. Furthermore, it does not negate the fact that Black people are twice as likely to be unemployed as white people nationwide.[20] In light of these inequities, it is little wonder then that with some regularity, the US experiences surges in protest and struggle in the streets and on campuses. Statistics about people of color regarding student loan debt, the probability of being employed and owning a home, and the likelihood of unemployment lay bare the national reality of the key difference between generational wealth and merely having money. These numbers speak to the specific, shared lived realities that illuminate the much more numerous and formidable obstacles people face under systemic oppression. Often, these obstacles remain implicit unless further investigation is done about the multiple, intertwined challenges that reside underneath the melting pot narrative of opportunity and social mobility.

However, even while coloniality has stratified who is worthy of well-being and health, learning has happened. It has happened even as fugitive act, and there have been plentiful collective movements for freedom and joy. Despite the ongoing spectacle of anti-Black murderous practices by law enforcement, now readily viewed through mandated body cameras in many police departments, Black people have loved, lived, found joy, and as the common saying goes, made a way out of no way.[21] Although the words that "all men are created equal" were written and co-signed by white men who actively engaged in the practice of owning other human beings and rendering Black people as property, Black people have fought hard and steady to make the words of equality true. It has always been and continues to be a struggle born of love and desire for freedom despite ongoing difficulties to simply live, let alone thrive.[22]

As the middle class has shrunk, and income disparity has reached record levels in the United States, obtaining a college degree has become more of a requirement for entry-level positions in the private and public sectors.[23] However, entry to, and persistence through, higher education often involves struggle for historically marginalized populations, including those students who fall short of the implicit ideal because they are not white, not cisgender, not able, and not male. Systemic racism in higher education has been well documented through extensive research, including *Transcending the Talented Tenth* by critical theorist Joy James, higher education scholar Dafina-Lazarus Stewart's blistering essay on the appeasement language of inclusion and diversity that does not discuss power, and historian Robin D. G. Kelley's careful examination of the history of freedom movements.[24] However, what is often overlooked is how settler colonialism has been baked into the structures of the United States, including higher education. When we limit our understanding of student protest to racism, we overlook both the breadth and depth of how inequities operate through many vehicles in higher education. Moreover, we miss the core of learning, including education for the purposes of struggle, as a profoundly human and humanizing endeavor, defiant and, when necessary, fugitive from the mechanisms of formal education.

Historically, the right to enter higher education has been reserved for the more privileged in society, at the expense of those purposefully excluded from full humanity so that their value was equated to their labor to raise cash crops and build infrastructure in the form of schools, railways, and more. The nation's oldest and most elite institutions of learning were created exclusively for land-owning white men. Those same institutions were built by enslaved labor. Historian Craig Steven Wilder's book *Ebony and Ivy* provides a careful and sobering history of the use of enslaved people's labor to build the country's most heralded colleges and universities, such as Harvard and Brown.[25] Even the nation's public institutions have similarly exclusive practices in place, such as application criteria that value SAT and GRE scores, particularly scores for mathematical aptitude, over qualitative data, often in the form of letters of recommendation from teachers who have spent countless hours with applicants. This tells us something about how a more detailed set of knowledge drawn from teacher-student relationships is simply valued less than scores on exams founded on Eurocentric norms and forms of knowledge. This is not to say that large-scale data are not important. Rather, the overreliance on one form of assessment leans into its Eurocentric subjects, even Eurocentric frames of seemingly neutral subject areas like chemistry and math. Institutions of higher education, particularly those seeking high status, render themselves servile to the rankings of the *U.S. News & World Report*'s annual list of "best" colleges that prioritizes GRE scores in its calculus. That this ranking by a conservative-leaning publication weighs considerably more than the knowledge of these students' teachers and communities reinforces not just what counts as knowledge but also who determines that in admissions and rankings.

In essence, it matters what a K–12 education provides students in preparing them for what they will encounter in large lecture courses in college. It matters that some young people know what a FAFSA is, which colleges might actively recruit them, and which histories and struggles have come before, particularly for students of color, in gaining access to a college education, including social networks that may prove crucial in their careers. While, at first glance, it might be tempting to attribute not knowing what a FAFSA is, for example, to families' and parents' lack of dedication to their children's education, the plain fact is that who knows these pathways and connections has far less to do with actual merit and dedication than with the well-tread patterns of cultural, economic, and social positioning.[26] If you are the college-educated parent of a child, and you hold a salaried job that affords you work-hour flexibility, the chances are much higher that your child will be in contact with the shared cultural and procedural practices of universities. Considering, then, the realities of privilege and the deprivation of knowledge and capital resources, it should not surprise us that whenever the doors to higher education have been widened for historically marginalized peoples, it has involved struggle.

The college campus protests of the 1960s spoke back to the racism across the nation and the Eurocentric nature of the college curriculum, as well as offering a sharp critique of the United States' military involvement in other nations, including the Vietnam War. As Kelley noted in his analysis of the ways that struggle for rights has necessarily involved political study, these struggles for freedom stretch far beyond the US. The tide of protests presented a challenge to universities, as they continue to do in the early twenty-first century. University administrators, in response to the campus protests in the 1960s, responded with the creation of Black studies, ethnic studies, and women and gender studies departments. The administrators of those years faced several challenges in taking action given several dynamics at play: the strength of student protests, the interests of boards of trustees that were and remain largely composed of white men, and the reality of the uprisings beyond US borders in which other nations liberated themselves from colonial rule. Alongside these protests, corporations were also turning to minority representation as a marketing strategy. The powers in higher education had no choice but to respond to students' demands for more inclusive admissions and shifts in curriculum.

Amid these varying and varied political mobilizations, universities responded through university channels: creating departments. These departments have created spaces for students to learn about history beyond the well-worn, Eurocentric national narratives. And they have reshaped how history itself is studied, altering it from the banking model of education indicted by Paulo Freire decades ago, an approach that treats students as vessels into which a curriculum can be deposited. Instead of treating education as a type of transition, these departments and their faculty, usually from minoritized populations, treat learning as an active, often collective, inquiry into knowledge systems and how they foster different relationships among the lifeforms of humans, land, sky, and waterways.[27] These same departments have also had to wrestle with university bureaucracies that have largely been and remain led by white men and women. In his book *The Reorder of Things*, Roderick Ferguson carefully documents how these same departments are often in the most precarious position on campus.[28] He makes the case that by the very position of being gifted into existence by the university, Black studies, ethnic studies, and other fields that deliberately focus on the struggles and victories of oppressed peoples are held back from manifesting their revolutionary potential. Instead, they are consumed by the machinery of higher education, which often includes endless debates about the rigor of fields outside of Eurocentric humanities and science.

In the early 1970s, this academic hand-wringing came in the form of debates about whether the quality of education would suffer as a result of another structural change in higher education: the creation of an open admissions policy, first pioneered at City College, one of the City University of New York's campuses. That policy was created in 1969 as a concession to a two-week-long protest in which Puerto Rican and Black students decried the school's overwhelmingly white student composition. They blocked the entrance to City College and demanded an open admissions policy. Some younger faculty members, including June Jordan and Adrienne Rich, now regarded as legendary Black feminist public intellectuals, joined the student resistance. The open admissions policy both led to material change for otherwise excluded Black and Puerto Rican students and created a new vehicle of monitoring and delimiting students' practices—and more pointedly, the practices of their institutions. Ferguson explains that, two years after the open admissions policy was implemented, City College would "graduate the largest number of black and Latino students with master's degrees [in New York], far outshining its larger sibling institution, the State University of New York. For some, open admissions would be a corruption of academic standards, and for others it would represent the democratization of higher education." Ferguson goes on to explain that "excellence" became an arbiter through which the legitimacy of the open admissions policy and, more fundamentally, meritocracy was reintroduced as a response to diversifying its student and faculty ranks. Academic institutions have become excellent and fluent in asking people to police their own excellence or worth, a point also articulated in Ferguson's work. This means that the revolutionary, transformative potential of ethnic studies departments, along with women's and gender studies departments, is dampened by a bureaucratic preoccupation with class size minimums, time spent in committees that are created for the ongoing disciplinary and culturally reproductive processes of curriculum review for the eyes of a largely white and male university administration, and ongoing deliberation about the research done by faculty in these departments to determine if it "counts" as knowledge.

Together, practices that question some forms of excellence, while always assuming other departments to be beyond reproach, contain and enclose the potential for deep transformation and even revolt for an education system that is by the people, for the people. Higher education has long been both a construct of colonialism and a hierarchy. The hierarchy, in which only those who have ascended through the long-standing cultural norms can weigh in on who is admitted, hired, and tenured, reproduces the hierarchy. More fundamentally, when minoritized peoples are allowed to enter, even in positions of power, the power relations in the university, including the board of trustees and budgetary control, remains unchanged. In the 1970s, the language of "excellence" was used to question the validity of the presence of minoritized people and their ways of knowing. In the late twentieth and early twenty-first century, articulations of diversity and inclusion perform similar functions: they proclaim a dedication for diversity but hold at bay substantive change to unhouse whiteness in higher education.[29]

Study and struggle have not happened asynchronously. In fact, study has been an essential part of various groups' protests and struggle to gain access to formal institutions of learning. For example, before the establishment of the student-run Black Action Society at the University of Pittsburgh, Black students collectively read critical analyses about racism through the poetry of Nikki Giovanni, and learned about pan-Africanism through the writings of Ghana's first president, Kwame Nkrumah. These readings were not available to them in their university library, but they found them in independent bookstores in traditionally Black neighborhoods in Pittsburgh. In the 1940s, long before these formations in the US, Black Caribbean communist Claudia Jones organized and founded two of the Black British community's foremost outlets for Black reading groups, the *West Indian Gazette* and *Afro-Asian Times*. These publications were products of political education and allowed for the creation study groups by and for Black Caribbean people living in the US and Great Britain. Africana studies and literature scholar Carole Boyce-Davies has curated and narrated the wide-ranging works of Claudia Jones that were both pivotal in communist organizing and yet overlooked in the recognition Jones received. Recovering the span of Jones's organizing work that centered on writing for the purpose of political education, and education for the purpose of ascertaining prevailing power dynamics, Boyce-Davies writes: "She made her presence felt in ways so remarkable that only conversations with friends who understand the blurring that exists between the worlds which we inhabit could appreciate."[30]

The protests that started on college campuses in 2015 and continued into 2020 are directly related to the protests that erupted in the streets after the murders of Trayvon Martin, Michael Brown, Tamir Rice, Sandra Bland, Philando Castile, Breonna Taylor, and George Floyd, to name just a few of the many Black lives cut short by overt legal and extralegal violence. The protests took the form of walkouts from classes at a coordinated time, vigils in the evenings, and die-ins that simulated the spectacle of the body of Michael Brown left for hours after a white police officer ended his life with gunfire. As with most uprisings, the protests came with demands. For example, the student activists at the University of North Carolina at Chapel Hill demanded several actions, including the removal of the university's statue of "Silent Sam," a mythic figure created to symbolize and romanticize the Confederacy's investment in an economy based on slavery. In 2017, the Afrikan Student Union at the University of California, Los Angeles, released a public statement of demands to the administration, including the allocation of $40 million toward an endowment for housing and sustaining a Black Resource Center, a place where the students could seek refuge from the racist harm they had experienced on campus.[31] The group's leaders pointed out that they were issuing their demand fifty-one years after the formation of the Afrikan Student Union, and that in that span, their experiences of anti-Black racism on campus had not substantively changed from their elders' experiences.

As with the nation in general, not only do colleges have a racism problem—more precisely an anti-Blackness problem—but they've had this problem from their inception, and not by accident. These institutions promote, through affinity groups for students of color and their public relations materials, the notion that racial advancement has already been achieved. These presentations shield them from the realities of persistent racism. This is, in part, why student protests occur. While each context is specific, with its own history preceding the moment protests make the newspaper headlines, the persistent evasions of profound change in higher education yield predictable uprisings.

The Emancipation Proclamation freed enslaved peoples, and the protests of the 1960s led to the vanquishing of racist "separate but equal" laws and policies. However, the struggle and study for freedom is both much richer in detail and more consistent in practice. As one pivotal example, *Black Reconstruction in America*, by the sociologist and social theorist W. E. B. Du Bois, points out to readers that the first major strike in the United States was conducted by enslaved peoples.[32] This strike was impossible without sharing knowledge and planning for resistance. However, anti-Black racism occludes knowledge of such early and powerful struggles for freedom in the United States.

Anti-Black racism is a crucial component of the ways that the United States maintains a colonialist structure. Although national narratives speak of manifest destiny and racial progress, these are in fact, at best, arguable when so many Black lives are ended by law enforcement and self-appointed guardians of the law. These narratives also hold little water when Native nations still strive for and enact sovereignty on their ancestral lands. Moreover, when racial advancement is overly focused on the United States, students and society at large are deprived of knowledge about resistance to colonization in myriad locations, such as Taîno princess Anacaona's resistance to Christopher Columbus's plundering and rape of Haiti as well as that Black nation's revolt for its independence from France. Student protests call us to reckon with the ongoing realities of sanctioned narratives that bely the messier reality of confronting the nation's ongoing history of profiting from enslaved labor that tilled wealth and created buildings on stolen land.

There are also important subtleties to the ways that settler colonialism has shaped epistemology, what counts as knowledge, and educational policy and practice via the emphasis on individual achievement. The simple fact that terms like "achievement," and, of course, the "achievement gap" are still widely used illustrates the ways that individual achievement is discussed and valued more than collective learning and well-being. Myopic focus on individual achievement blurs our ability to apprehend systemic obstacles and advantages that produce inequity based on race, gender, sexual identity, class, and forms of ability. For example, the long-standing and uninterrupted interconnectedness among all living beings in Indigenous epistemologies is regularly erased. Even in environmental activist circles, land is rarely conceived as being a living entity with a sacred essence, and people seldom discuss how human beings have had many forms of spiritual connections to land, water, and air.[33]

An example where this interconnectedness was missing is the Global Climate Strike, held on September 20, 2019. Organizers estimated that on that Friday, four million children and young people were in the streets on every continent, calling for the cessation of climate change harms that they were positioned to inherit.[34] While the call to change and for world leaders to take responsibility for future generations was certainly a success in terms of its size and clear message, only in a few locations did protesters discuss land and Indigeneity. This is even more striking when considering the strong, extended Dakota Access Pipeline protests at the Standing Rock Indian Reservation beginning in 2016. As part of establishing a site for the Water Protectors, learning was a necessity. Mní Wičhóni Nakíčižiŋ Owáyawa, The Defenders of the Water School, was located in the Očhéthi Šakówiŋ Camp at Standing Rock. The school was created by Alayna Eagle Shield, a Lakota language specialist. And at the time of this writing, the school remains in existence, providing resources to Native parents whose children can maintain their learning about and through traditional Indigenous ways of knowing. This act of prioritizing relational learning, though, fell under the radar of most mainstream media outlets, and if history is any predictor, is unlikely to be noted in K–12 history textbooks that address this particular example of resistance and study.

Colonialism has, instead, specific ideas for what counts and how to achieve success. For example, when achievement is upheld as the key standard rather than learning, it brings with it a toolkit of measurements, remediation programs, expulsion policies, and merito-cratic explanations of who achieves and how. The federal education policies No Child Left Behind and Race to the Top, versions one and two all echo the idea of linear improvement while pursuing and lauding competition and individualized achievement.

Movements of protest and struggle, in their many different shapes, have included study. This phenomenon preceded the oft-referenced civil rights movement, dating back to struggles of communist activists in the early twentieth-century South. As Robin D. G. Kelley documents in *Hammer and Hoe*, the Alabama Communist Party, composed largely of poor Black workers and some white allies, pushed a multifaceted agenda for relief from racism, classism, and patriarchy.[35] Although the majority of people in this collective would be deemed semi-literate in a strict sense of the word, they still managed to study together, in churches and then through wider organizing groups, with the goal of exchanging ideas and forging collectives for action. Although the specific contexts of time and place are deeply important to each movement for justice, it is also important to note that movements of study and struggle can also serve as palimpsests across movements.

The contemporary Black Lives Matter movement has been calling out militarized anti-Black police brutality, a pervasive racist culture, and the ongoing pillage of the land for profit. On the face of it, this movement seems to have sprung up spontaneously, but as with most collective demands for justice, people have engaged in study to formulate their arguments, demands, and practices. An example of this study is found in the platform issued by the Movement for Black Lives.[36] Black Lives Matter is a large, decentralized social protest. From these protests, the Movement for Black Lives coalesced from several coalitions to continually study and provide political education and policy demands for Black lives. The platform, launched in 2016 and since then revised on an ongoing basis, begins with the over-arching first plank, "End the War on Black People."[37] It includes several policy demands, among them the end to the surveillance of Black youth and the assault on Black women. The demands, which number more than a dozen, are presented as intertwined, meaning that addressing just one vector of oppression is incomplete and inconsistent with how oppression works through multiple delivery systems. One of the most poignant points is a call for the end to equating violations of property with the extinguishing of human life. Throughout the platform's references to struggle, that act is not equated with "looting," which the platform deftly dismisses without ever giving the racialized use of that word any space. The platform itself is a form of public pedagogy, one that is specific, freely available, and constantly edited and informed by collective gatherings to address the nuances of the assault on Blackness.

In social movements throughout history, out of necessity, study and struggle have been intimately linked. In the 1960s, the Student Nonviolent Coordinating Committee (SNCC) prioritized debating every single action in group meetings.[38] From deciding how to understand communities and their disenfranchisement to how to raise interest and willingness to risk physical harm for the right to vote, every decision was debated and often informed by shared readings of radical thinkers SNCC had undertaken as a group. For example, when someone approached SNCC proposing to photograph their actions, the group debated their reservations about how the photographs would be used and the value of having their work made more visible. This debate was within the context of SNCC's commitment to archiving their work to ensure its accuracy and impact. Just about any person can register for a New York public library card; sign up for a time to read through Ella Baker's papers, housed in the Schomburg Center for Black Studies; and for no fee, learn from the minutes of SNCC. This access is itself a political act, an opening to learn, free of tuition charge, lab fees, and credit requirements. As stated throughout the online digital archive of SNCC (also freely available), the organization also used photography to provide incontrovertible evidence that their approach to social transformation was to learn about the everyday lives of those whose civil rights were restricted through various racist codes. How SNCC walked alongside people was a mode of organizing itself, and their documentation of this is an act of public pedagogy.[39] What is not so readily available in the online archives, though, is the robust debate about whom the organization should receive funding from and how they should receive it. These debates are documented, in line-by-line transcriptions of SNCC's meetings, also housed in the Schomburg Center. They shed light on how the SNCC was primarily focused on civil rights, particularly the right to vote, but also how the group discussed many facets of the nation and the globe, including the movements happening in nations far away. In other words, they studied racism and colonialism as ways to inform their actions.

SNCC members read and discussed classic works by the first prime minister and president of Ghana, the pan-Africanist Kwame Nkrumah, the scholar and educator Carter G. Woodson, and Harriet Tubman, with a focus on her practices of literally stealing back Black lives from slavery. They researched the areas of the nation where particular obstacles made it all but impossible for Black Americans to vote. For the members of SNCC, the research led to empirical knowledge of how the daily activities of Black Southerners included spaces of ease and, more poignantly, barriers to voting and enacting their civil rights. For many Black and Chicanx student groups in the 1960s, political study was first about achieving self-determination, in both the individual and collective sense, and achieving self-edification in an anti-Black settler state. These investigations often led to further study that helped to connect the struggles of marginalized peoples in the United States to those living in other colonized states. Important work by W. E. B. Du Bois and

Claudia Jones consistently connected economic power structures across nations, particularly in their impacts on Black peoples on the African continent and beyond.[40]

An important component of the study pursued by these groups involved working closely alongside different peoples, with whom they shared many racialized and gendered identities. For contemporary social movements on college campuses, much of joining together and organizing has come through the dissonance, if not harm, that BIPOC, as students, experience encountering the curricula, symbols, and building names that herald deceased men who oppressed their ancestors. Many scholars and activists have cautioned against submitting political demands through stories of pain, as it is far too easy and common for colleges to respond by prescribing listening sessions and not making material changes. However, it is also true that when student activists decry statues and building names, it challenges whose history has been concretized as objective and central, as well as challenging the colonizing process through which knowledge is sanctified. When minoritized students are asked to learn from largely Eurocentric knowledges, they are rightfully dismayed at discovering what, precisely, they have signed up for. An approach to study that is at once disruptive and grounding, and often extends beyond higher education's curriculum, has meant and should mean many things. When students of varying class, race, gender, ability, and sexual identity come into contact with a form of study that moves away from the well-worn myths, of the nation and world, they undergo a significant transformation in how they understand themselves in relation to the world. A lingering question is, when white students from middle- and upper-middle-class homes experience learning that disrupts the narratives they've been told about meritocracy and the American dream, what follows?

Although understanding systemic racism addresses some questions about the treatment that BIPOC, queer, and working poor students experience on campus, understanding settler colonialism leads to a different set of questions: How could study not involve struggle for those in a nation forged through theft of land, in an economy based on racist capitalism, and amid the ongoing attempt to erase Indigeneity? Why are existing relationships to land and neighborhoods rarely discussed in the proposals to expand large universities in urban areas? Why and how is heteropatriarchy perpetuated through curriculum and through campus cultures? What is the relationship between Native sovereignty and Black freedom struggles? Most fundamentally, how has colonialism limited our very idea of achievement and what it means to study in formal education spaces? It has, in essence, told us the lie that the information taught in various disciplines contains objective facts, impermeable and without context. That lie has provided opportunity and access for a precious few. Settler colonialism has attempted to commodify knowledge itself, anointing it as property, convertible into careers and well-being.

Understanding settler colonialism as an ongoing structure provides a more robust route to understanding how various populations experience distinct but deeply connected forms of marginalization from formal institutions in the United States, including higher education. Those distinct forms of marginalization explain why gaining access to study has had to involve both internal political education and external public teachings, with attempts to shift the shared imaginary and material realities for Native peoples.

In 2018, 23 percent of Native Americans and Alaska Natives ages eighteen to twenty-four were enrolled in college, compared with 57 percent of white youth enrolled.[41] While there had been significant growth of Native Indians and Alaska Natives enrolled between 2008 and 2015, those numbers have dwindled in recent years. Within that enrollment, there were roughly three times as many Native women as men, a gap roughly two times greater than the gender gap for Black Americans. These statistics and history matter when we pause to remember that every postsecondary institution of learning sits upon what was once sovereign Indigenous land, often under a matriarchal system. And what is arguably more important, that land was treated as a relation—as ancestor, elder, parent, child—not as property. This thirst for ownership is a concerning trend, and part of what has created a culture of property and uneven power in higher education, dating back to the Morrill Acts of the nineteenth century, which parceled out seized Indigenous lands from the federal government to establish land grant institutions, a complex web of commodification further explored in chapter 2. Should they be admitted to institutions of higher education, students from marginalized communities often face tricky challenges of navigating institutions that have excluded them and their histories but also desperately want to not be seen as racist. As a result, students have to deal with what is colloquially referred to as the "tax" they must pay as part of their admission to higher education: be visible and speak for your entire race or culture.

Lumbee Tribe member and professor Bryan McKinley Jones Brayboy has written eloquently about the hypervisibility that American Indian students experience in Ivy League settings. In a well-known article entitled "Hiding in the Ivy," Brayboy details the ways three Native students in the 1990s navigated their Ivy League institutions, and weaves the complicated threads of being both visible and invisible.[42] Brayboy juxtaposes their cultural integrity with the ongoing suppression of Native sovereignty and presents the way these students sometimes use invisibility as a buffer against the negative impacts that come with being visible, or more specifically, hypervisible. "Hypervisiblity" is not a term that Brayboy uses, but the close and focused attention on these students—part fear, part fascination, part suspicion—creates for them an experience that is at once hypervisible and hypervigilant. As a result, they can be scrutinized more, asked to speak on behalf of all Native peoples, or assumed to be in a greater need of remediation than the rest of the college population. This aspect of being watched is why many Native students, as Brayboy notes in one of the opening illustrations in the article, will literally take longer, less-popular walking routes to certain buildings in order to materially and psychically protect themselves.

While Brayboy doesn't use the term "struggle" or raise it as a theme, there are both elements of tension and careful engagement in how Native American and Alaska Native students navigate post-secondary institutions. In fact, read from the lens of study and struggle, it is clear how the students profiled in the article studied their campuses as a way to navigate them.

Brayboy's points about the psycho-emotional and material costs of hypervisibility are helpful in understanding ongoing abuses of power that happen even before students apply to colleges. In April 2018 two young Mohawk men were late joining a tour of Colorado State University (CSU), having had some difficulty finding the starting location. After they found the group, within minutes, a white mother who described herself as "nervous" on the tour called the police, reporting two "suspicious looking" youths.[43] The incident itself speaks volumes about who is seen to belong and who, at a moment's glance, is seen as other and criminally suspect. In education research, Native youth are too often seen as always at risk or victims. In this case, though, it was a white woman whose safety was made questionable, by her perceptions. That perception then made the two young people suspicious and questionable. It echoes the murder of Trayvon Martin by a self-appointed neighborhood watchperson and his description of Martin as looking "suspicious," as well as the killing of Michael Brown by the white police officer Darren Wilson and his description of Brown as a "monster." I raise this point to again show how universities practice the same anti-Black racist and colonizing patterns that are found outside of campuses.

However, there is promise in the moments when the truth is told. In a sobering and unique public response, then president of CSU Tony Frank issued a formal apology to the two young Mohawk men, writing that "anyone who is 'uncomfortable with a diverse and inclusive academic environment' should find another campus elsewhere."[44] Frank's apology and stance about inclusivity stands out from many college administration reactions to incidences of racism, or to student protests against racism that treat the inciting incident as a singular and unfortunate occurrence. In the spring and summer of 2020, following and during the global uprising against white police killings of Black peoples, dozens upon dozens of university presidents and provosts penned public letters. Notably, the 2020 collection of public statements often named anti-Black racism as an ill that universities needed to face, a far more specific and accurate assessment than the typical phrasing offering diversity and inclusion as the solution to all structural obstacles relating to race. Tony Frank used the word "inclusion" but evaded the reasons why campuses have been selectively inclusive rather than transformative. The statements penned in 2020 following the killings of George Floyd and Breonna Taylor also stopped short of identifying the role that campus police play as part of the national power structure surveillance and abuse that is protected through impunity for police officers, school safety officers, and immigration enforcement officers.

Perhaps even more tellingly, higher education still speaks in terms of diversity, equity, and inclusion. In my two-year stint as an associate dean for equity and justice, I learned many things, including that there was a name for people in this type of position, with people shifting rapidly in these positions and without the funding to make substantive power shifts. We held DEI positions: the acronym stood for "diversity, equity, and inclusion." The acronym and the words it stood for made me bristle, and still do. "Diversity" asks how many of which categories are present on any given campus. "Equity," while important, is rarely defined and therefore left glaringly insufficient. Most concerning to me was "inclusion." That was then and remains today a profoundly passive and analytically weak term to use. Inclusion is irreconcilable with the foundational hierarchy and surveillance that higher education rests on. In order for higher education to be more inclusive, it would actually need to reckon with its history, its origins, and the ongoing nature of colonization and transform its ways of being. More specifically, the ivory tower and those paid by it, including me, need to consider seriously how we are with each other, how we deem some knowledge systems canon to the exclusion of others, and how, when we refer to "the community"—as we often do—we mean, apparently, everyone who is not of the university. Singular references to "the community" reveal how researchers regard varied peoples and histories. Do we speak to perform our intelligence? Do we research and publish to reap the oft-discussed rewards of tenure, which is increasingly voided of its promise of academic freedom? How do we mentor graduate students and junior faculty in a way that doesn't reach for tenure but instead grounds their humanness in learning alongside people? How are we with the histories and contemporary dynamics of extraction and violence that run deep? How are we with the discomfort at our reckoning with our own complicity, outside of running immediately away from it? These questions require action in the form of transformation, also known as learning. Inclusion is a softer term and asks for much less. Although it may not ever find its way into mainstream history textbooks, it was Dr. Martin Luther King Jr.— beloved and, in US textbooks, also whitewashed—who, toward the end of his far-too-short life, questioned his own Christian-informed leadership for integration, wondering if he had been advocating for inclusion into a "burning house."

The "nervous" mother who called the police during the CSU college tour, out of a misplaced perception of threat, was doing so because this nation continues to materially protect and perpetuate the well-being of white people to the exclusion of all other groups. She had been socialized to believe the lie that youth of color, particularly when transgressing a rule regarding timeliness, were to be held in suspicion, subject to arrest, for her literal and imagined safety. She was socialized by not just those lies but the widely held love of those lies. That grotesque love is what has shaped the US and helped it continue its legacy of stolen land on stolen labor through carceral practices for profit that impact marginalized communities beginning in K–12 education and even before. How are we with the fact that kindergarteners can be expelled from school, as education researcher and liberatory activist Carla Shalaby asks us? The hard facts are that the nation was founded on stolen labor on stolen land. Higher education thrives on that foundation and ongoing project. If not addressed directly, it will only continue that pattern. Every social movement that has addressed higher education directly has, in fact, had close relationships with these truths of higher education. Confronting those truths is, in part, what allowed study and action groups to transcend the very enclosures it has created for them.

> If now is not a good time to tell the truth, then I
> don't see when we'll get to it.
>
> —NIKKI GIOVANNI[45]

To contend with the complexities of the ongoing reality and truth of settler colonialism, several grounding principles are crucial. First and foremost, formal education has always been part of the settler colonial structure of this nation—from its birth in the form of Ivy League schools, exclusive and steeped in Eurocentric knowledge written by and for white men, to the ways that land and labor have literally been stolen to build land grant institutions. The academy is a strident hierarchy, in which only those at the top of the ranks have a say in the promotion and retention of more junior faculty. For example, in a deliberation about whether an assistant professor should be promoted and granted tenure, it typically only involves those that have tenure, regardless of their expertise in that particular candidate's area of expertise. This process does several things. It reinforces an established culture that reproduces itself by advancing those who look, act, and talk in ways that are recognizable to tenured faculty. More simply put, people in power sanction those who appear familiar. As a result, the highest rank of full professor is still overwhelmingly white and male. Black women make up less than 3 percent of all full professors, meaning that the tenured professoriate is largely unable to grasp the intertwined patriarchy and anti-racism that Black female professors face. It's a logic of worth that has been defined by people who often come from homes where family members hold advanced degrees, and college is not only taken for granted, but even described in detail in terms of one's major and the school they attended. Similarly, the nation has used logics regarding who is more and less human to justify labor exploitation and the seizure of land. When those truths are not spoken, we are in essence preserving the credentials and means of ascendance for the dominant population. And we are co-signing education systems that tell BIPOC that their stories are either inferior or simply do not exist.

Second, and critically important, marginalized populations have never ceded learning and study for the few at the top. As long as there has been conquest and delineation between those who are less and more worthy of life, there have been struggles and projects of self-determination.[46] Study in the form of political education is essential because it involves not just study but the specific study of power relations and how they might be altered through collective action. Study, in fact, often includes struggle, grappling with ideas and practices in the pursuit of freedom—a far cry from "diversity and inclusion." This form of study has been essential to the struggle to gain access to study further. In fact, there is no divide between political struggle and study. They interlope, intertwine, and depend on each other.

CHAPTER TWO

SETTLER COLONIALISM

When Dulani Muhammad (a pseudonym) and I met in her junior year of high school to catch up, we talked about school, family, crushes, and much in between. I had known this slight young woman since she was fourteen years old and newly arrived to the United States from Iran. When I asked her about how she was faring during college application season, her brow furrowed and she rolled her eyes.

"I just really wish it were over. It's the only thing anybody talks about. I want to jump forward and be wherever we are going to be and get on with it," she said.

An ardent student, she is the kind of young person who has juggled three AP classes with staggering workloads, cooked dinner for her grandmother after school until her parents returned from their jobs at a local convenience store, and never lost step with her friends via text messages and social media. Part of her exasperation is owed to the expanse that she has to bridge between the sweeping dreams she carries as the daughter of migrants and the detailed energies and worries of belonging and identity she negotiates with her college-going peers. What she also expressed that day was her sense of unease with writing about herself for the college essays. She knew that it worked in her favor to write about her journey, particularly the portions that held pain, but she was also sharp enough to know that this depiction collapsed her full humanity more than enlivened her worries and passions. Some of her passions had to do with migration, workers' rights, and women, all issues that many would assume to be "hers" as a young brown woman in the United States. And others simply did not match up with her demographic profile, such as her insightful analysis of the exploitation of Black men through professional sports. When it came time to write her essay, Dulani made a bargain. She wrote about her experiences as a young Muslim female who didn't yet have the precise words to articulate the experience of depicting herself through the lens that society uses to see portions of her it prefers to see, specifically resilience through victimhood. In the year after submitting that application, Dulani would go on to gain much more insight that, in both productive and discomforting ways, complicating how she understood herself in terms of the implicit and explicit desires she and others held for college life and life itself.

In 1996, the year Dulani was born, the tuition and fees at what would become her dream school, Harvard University, were $26,575 a year.[1] By the spring of 2016, Harvard's tuition and fees had soared to $59,550.[2] Accounting for inflation, this is an increase of almost $20,000. Harvard is far from unique or even an outlier in this sharp increase in tuition. What is perhaps just as telling as the increased costs and profit-driven investments in higher education is the steady increase in enrollment during these years. And while college enrollment and debt have increased, rates of employment, home ownership, and career stability have become more precarious, particularly for young people of color.[3] Although it is assumed that everyone should go to college, it is far from clear what the nation and the world receives from there being more people enrolled. Criticism ranges from indicting the liberal politics that tend to predominate on college campuses to the skyrocketing costs of increasingly privatized higher education. While politicians consistently support agendas of college for all, they fail to appreciate all sorts of histories—both historical and contemporary, fiscal and cultural.

In 2015, Dulani graduated from high school and enrolled in a private, liberal arts college in the Northeast. Although it was not her dream school, she blossomed in many ways. She grew as a thinker, and with that, grew increasingly dissatisfied with what a hegemonically white university and country implicitly wanted from her. The hesitations she expressed while she was in high school could be articulated in bolder detail once she was living and studying at a predominantly white campus. She participated in two protests during the spring of 2016, her first year as a student, decrying entrenched racism on campus. They were led by students of color, mostly Black students in their junior and senior years. When I talked to her at the end of that first year, she said she felt both more and less able to speak about herself. As she put it, "Sometimes I can speak so loudly and have my friends to keep me company, and then other times, especially in classes, I feel like I can't speak at all, like it's all stuck in my throat."[4]

There are many ways that Dulani and students like her, racially minoritized students, are asked to be both present and not present on university campuses.[5] Although this may seem impossible—how can one be both visible and invisible?—it is a phenomenon that many writers of color have addressed, including Ralph Ellison in his novel *Invisible Man*. In the novel, a Black man struggles with being invisible as a human in a white-dominated society, and also with the visibility that being criminalized brings. Relatedly, in classroom discussions about race, students of color are hyper-visible, often asked to speak on behalf of a singular, mythic "minority" experience. I have experienced this myself as a student at K–12 and higher education levels. On the first day of my ninth-grade geography class, in a majority-white school, the teacher had been proceeding smoothly through roll call until she called my name and then abruptly stopped. She asked me if I was from India. I nodded, wanting the conversation to end there and for her to return to her roll call of students. Instead, she told me, and the class, that she had recently visited India and love, love, loved it. She asked if I could bring in some "traditional food and maybe even some of [my] mother's traditional clothing" sometime? I skipped that class for the next two weeks. This is a small example of singling someone out by making a whole suite of assumptions and collapsing the nuances of their culture. A superficial—and incorrect—understanding might call this "culturally relevant teaching," but truly relevant teaching requires knowing learners and their experiences. This cannot be ascertained merely from surnames, phenotypes, or how people perform their gender.

Unsurprisingly, these issues of conflating superficial features with knowledge shows up in professional interactions. During the first few years in my work as a college professor, a white male colleague stopped me in the hallway to ask if I read an ethnographic study of youth in the Goa region of India. I had not read the article and asked him why he was asking me about it. It would never have crossed my mind to show him an article about white male professors in the South and if he could provide me an opinion about its validity. These are the ways in which BIPOC are asked to speak for all in their perceived ethnic group and, simultaneously, endure the erasure of the specifics of their experiences.

During many faculty meetings, I have heard faculty express wishes that students of color did not sit together during class. As Beverly Daniel Tatum so eloquently explained in her now-classic book, *Why Are All the Black Kids Sitting Together in the Cafeteria?*, they do so for the same reasons that the athletes might sit together, or the debate team, or the AP students.[6] Black students might be in all of those groups, but when they sit together, their decision to do so is questioned. It is a form of singling out collectivity that other groups are not asked to answer for. In higher education, students of color, many of whom may lack generational wealth but whose perceived cultural knowledges are solicited to be prominently featured in glossy brochures about diversity on campus, are disproportionately asked to provide input and even leadership on committees and task forces about racism on campus. They are treated, in a sense, as commodities. You might ask, "But isn't it a good thing to ask students for their input?" Certainly, but they are paying tuition to learn, not to provide uncompensated labor to faculty who are earning a much greater sum of money than some graduate students earn as stipends. They often also feel invisible, as they do not see themselves reflected in curricula of their college, its faculty, and, especially, its administrative ranks. Through student protests, many have articulated that these contradictory messages are inherent to being "diverse" on historically white campuses.

The desired narrative in college essays and Dulani's misgivings about that performance reveal a complexity about the implicit costs that Black and brown students bear. This is especially the case for those students who are the first in their family to attend college, and made to feel they have been given a gift. They receive the tacit idea that Black, Native, and brown bodies owe gaining entrance to college to someone else. In many studies, students of color have testified to the ways that they are all seen to be at the university by virtue of affirmative action.[7] The university is the creditor, and students of color are made to feel indebted. Also of note in this situation is who literally profits from the presence of students of color on college campuses and in society. Although universities that are predominantly white are keen to have their students and faculty of color featured prominently in their marketing materials, that representation upholds the image of a racially diverse and inclusive setting while reseating white patriarchal power. The images of diversity obscure the reality of who is admitted, who graduates, and, arguably most sobering, who is employed and free from student debt after graduation. This complicated mix of emotional and material debt also holds implications and determines material realities for both those who feel they belong on campus and those who don't. A gift economy positions some students as always being only minimally worthy of the beneficence of a university or other patriarchal entity, and it pervades the college-going experience of students from nondominant backgrounds, like Dulani, as well as college administrators who do the daily work of "gifting."

Gift economies are a colonial structure that imagines some people as worthy only through the benevolence of people with higher status. After initially praising the Indigenous peoples of this continent for their community and agricultural practices, European settlers quickly moved to narratives of savagery to justify the theft of land and the removal of newly deemed "savage" peoples from their lands.[8] These are the same narratives that justified the creation of the nation's most respected institutions of higher education, which also were open only to land-owning white man. Land grant universities, such as Pennsylvania State University, were established in the mid-1850s. They touted democracy and civic refinement, but did so with Indigenous lands stolen and recast as property for the benefit of land-owning white men.[9] Today's contradictions reflect a similar divergence between deed and practice. Students like Dulani enroll in higher education to further their learning and advance their life chances, but they are often surprised at the amount of unpaid labor they find themselves doing as "diverse" students. Little wonder that from time to time, the pervasive racism and erasure of Indigeneity connects to students' discordant experiences, and protests surge.

To understand the campus uprisings in the mid-to-late 2010s as reflective only of those years is a historical, political, and economic mistake. These protests, characterized by marches, die-ins, and sit-ins in university administrators' offices, are without a doubt connected to earlier protests, such as those of the 1960s and even earlier, but more fundamentally, they are connected to the history and structure of higher education within a stratified society. Dulani's first experiences of collective resistance put her in historical contact with not only uprisings of the past but also the particular manifestations of oppression that propelled these uprisings. Uprisings, though interconnected, are contextually specific, as racist capitalism has found many ways to shapeshift to maintain its power. Uprisings and riots are in a dynamic, dialectic relationship to the societal structure. Societies and its institutions, including higher education, reflect each other. Every single social and political space of the United States has been deeply shaped by the history and structure of empire and colonialism and, in turn, feeds back into those structures. However, none of these entities is definitively foreclosed from moments of connection, a flattening of hierarchies, and a radical love for freedom. The academy is no different and no less permeable than any other sector, including the legal and criminal justice systems, the health care system, organized labor, and K–12 education. While the impact of racism on higher education is indisputable, and, in many ways, yet to be fully comprehended, much less discussed is settler colonialism, even though it has been a part of higher education from the first universities.

While race is a construct, and racism is crucial to understanding how higher education is intertwined with practices the center capital and debt, settler colonialism offers a different lens. It provides an analytic structure that contends with anti-Black racism as well as the attempt to erase Indigeneity and the constant thrum of machinations to create property. Settler colonialism is a structure that arranges people relative to land, recast as property, and relative to each other, in the quest for empire. Settlers must always be settling land and turning it into property, Indigenous peoples must always be disappearing, Black peoples' humanity must always be in question, and forced migrants must always be denied their legitimacy as humans.[10] These intertwined practices create relationships among people and to knowledge, status, and therefore learning in the United States. As demonstrated by the Mexican American studies program in Tucson, Arizona, and ethnic studies programs in California, when high school students' learning goes beyond the Eurocentric curriculum, particularly when they learn about their cultural heritage and histories, they benefit in many ways, including feeling a connection to narratives in which they are not the conquered or the disappeared.[11] However, in both instances, there were popular and legal resistance to introducing histories of racially minoritized peoples into public school curricula. When students learn from primarily a Eurocentric curriculum, they are deprived of the many knowledge systems and traditions that have long existed before and alongside colonialism. White students are miseducated to believe that Eurocentric knowledge is objective truth writ large, and students of color experience disassociation from their varied cultural heritages. In her book *We Want to Do More Than Survive*, about the plight of Black children in what she terms the "educational survival complex," education scholar Bettina Love calls such cultural disassociation "spirit murder."[12]

Dulani's misgivings about writing her college application essay weren't just about being a young brown woman in a white-identified society, but how gifts and debts are implicitly tallied in the larger calculus of who has rightful access to higher education and who must ask for entry. The terms of inclusion are often understood through race, gender, and class, and sometimes sexual identity, but rarely in terms of how these categories create relationships to knowledge. As high school and college students' mobilizations have demonstrated, their struggle to learn about their histories beyond Eurocentric views and curriculum is "political." Students from any social category reading about the United States through the narrative of "discovery" is not political. These are the ways that curriculum itself is political, with those reflected in Eurocentric curricula affirmed in their social position, reinforcing the notion that white domination is merely undisputed reality. Countless reports and studies document the "achievement gap" that compare BIPOC students to white, and sometimes Asian students. When queer, poor, and dis/abled students, particularly those of color, mobilize for formal education to see them and their strengths, their struggles push past being categorized as at-risk. An understanding of settler colonialism puts these relationships to knowledge into relief by lifting up the inherent conflicts between learning and settler needs to establish property relations to knowledge, holding power by claiming some knowledge as "objective."

SETTLER COLONIALISM

The United States, as well as many other nations, including Australia, Canada, and Israel, has a society structured by settler colonialism.[13] Unlike a system based on extracting resources, goods, and human subjects from "other lands," settler colonialism is based on the logic of owning land, and that there is never enough land to satisfy the landowners' thirst.[14]

Land is the central organizing feature in settler colonialism, which has implications for all peoples' and life-forms' relationship to land and each other. In other forms of colonialism, domination can be established and maintained solely through the extraction of labor and resources. Most schoolchildren in the United States come into contact with the idea of colonialism through its subvariant term and concept, "colony." They learn the history of the United States, starting with the thirteen colonies, through high school history textbooks, including those released by major publishers like Houghton Mifflin, which replace the facts of European invasion with one about people fleeing England for religious freedom. This mythology of the nation's first founders then segues into a study of the American

Revolution and the cutting of ties to England. This is what led my sixth-grade teacher to think that a class field trip to Boston Harbor would bring to life what the British subjects were revolting against. In the narrative's tidy, linear sequence, Indigeneity is literally erased. After the Wôpanâak peoples—if they are even named specifically as such, rather than "Native" peoples—enjoyed a Thanksgiving meal with European settlers, they are not mentioned again. The omission makes it seem like the still very much alive and active Wôpanâak peoples simply vanished into the woods west of the Eastern seaboard. Moreover, the erasure is made more severe because the narrative associates colonialism with a bygone era, removed from contemporary society and its stories of progress, improvement, and development. When people learn about colonialism as a historical era, it renders opaque the colonial structure that is actively maintained in a settler-colonialist state.

John Gast's 1872 painting *American Progress* helps to demonstrate the important role that narratives perform in blurring the ongoing settler structure of society. The painting, often situated on US history textbook pages that discuss the doctrine of manifest destiny that justified westward expansion, depicts a vast landscape of the Western portion of the continent now called North America. On this land are small wagons, stagecoaches, and trains, extending in that order from the foreground to the background, to symbolize the sequence of technological progress. White male pioneers are marching and steering these vehicles, all looking toward the left edge of the painting, embodying westward expansion. Floating above the men and their wagons is a large, angel-like white woman, dressed in a flowing white dress, with blond hair wafting behind her. The woman is also looking westward and is holding a leather-bound book, entitled simply "School Book." Part of the cultural propaganda created in the 1800s to narratively justify the violent treatment of Indigenous peoples, this painting romanticizes expansion overseen by white men on behalf of inherent progress and for the benefit and protection of an angelic, pure white woman, reifying whiteness and gendered roles in the nation's creation. Notably, the painting leaves out the violence done to Indigenous peoples then and now, including the forced removal from lands through massacres and germ warfare.[15] The looming figure of the white Christian woman is deeply connected to this erasure, symbolically justifying settler patriarchal violence without a drop of red paint.

In fact, the plains depicted in Gast's painting were "home" to massive efforts to displace Native American tribes. Ten years before Gast painted this sweeping story of manifest destiny and European progress, a war broke out between European settlers and the Dakota peoples. On December 26, 1862, 38 Dakota men were marched to their deaths, in the largest mass hanging ever to take place on Turtle Island. An estimated four thousand spectators gathered to line the street as the men were marched to the specially constructed hanging platform. The 38 were part of a larger initial group of 303 sentenced to death for having participated in an uprising in Mankato Territory. The Dakota people had resisted being put on the brink of starvation as a result of treaty violations by the US government, which enabled settlers to flood the land and foodways of the once sparsely populated area. The uprising of the Dakota took place in response to a large-scale, armed settler encroachment. President Abraham Lincoln, the Great Emancipator, made the decision to hold the largest mass hanging to date to quell the uprising and, implicitly, calm settler anxieties and secure settler property entitlement. He reduced the number of Dakota men to be executed from 303 to 38. Lincoln explained the decision in an address to the US Senate:

> Anxious to not act with so much clemency as to encourage another outbreak on one hand, nor with so much severity as to be real cruelty on the other, I ordered a careful examination of the records of the

trials to be made, in view of first ordering the execution of such as had been proved guilty of violating females.

However, before the hangings took place, Lincoln's own examination of the transcripts and trials showed that only two men were convicted of rape. Lincoln then expanded his criteria for criminal guilt, from the original language of participation in "battles" to participation in "massacres," on top of the charges of rape, to fit the government's purpose of strategically containing a rightful backlash to settler encroachment. It is little wonder that Gast's painting, with its larger-than-life white woman floating above white male settlers, figures into the equation of the violent erasure of Indigeneity and Blackness, justified through the protection of white women.

Dakota scholar Kim Tallbear has called these shattering events of the 1860s the "origin story of the Dakota people today" because of the ways that the Dakota people have made meaning of their histories and contemporary lives in relation to them.[16] Without a doubt, Native peoples' origin stories do not involve colonialism, but Tallbear's point is that dealing with a state of ongoing occupation is a centuries-long reality for Native peoples.

Not coincidentally, the national profit gained through forced Black and Chinese labor is also absent from this image. The painting blurs the narrative of the settler colonialist project through both what is present and what is missing. When children and youth see this painting in their textbooks on pages introducing "Manifest Destiny," or "Westward Expansion," they implicitly learn that this time of expansion was both necessary and in the past. Functionally, this makes it much more difficult to indict the practice of stolen labor on stolen land that has been pivotal to this and all settler colonies. But the children viewing this image are not monolithic. A young white child may learn that this is a rather simple story, go on to play computer simulations of *The Oregon Trail*, and not think very much more about the terms of property and debt. An Indigenous child, though, or a Black one, may have an entirely different experience, one that pulls at complicated strings of being erased from a hyperbolic narrative. Or another white child may experience misgivings and uneasiness about the history's obvious omission of theft and violence, but may not have much guidance about what to do with the distorted curriculum, sanctioned by a largely white female field of teachers that has been miseducated to never know about these omissions, let alone how to address them with children and youth. This miseducation has long-term ramifications that often extend into college and that vary greatly for different groups—both for those (white and male) who have had a more straightforward relationship to education and experience it merely as a neutral place, and those for whom the terms of inclusion instill notions of inferiority and can always be revoked at any time. Relatedly, and at the root of Dulani's misgivings about her college application essay, is the question of how the terms of inclusion can be negotiated within a narrative that erases so much of the nation's violent practices in the interest of property accumulation for others.

As Sylvia Wynter has detailed, the larger colonial project has its genealogical roots in determining which lands, skies, and waterways were deemed holier, better, and higher. Being able to name a land as civilized endowed certain humans with the right to make these distinctions. Wynter referred to these ongoing practices as "knowledge for" projects: knowledge for domination and knowledge for ownership.[17] By proxy, that process of elevating certain land for ownership also held immediate implications regarding which beings were deemed to be human and which were not. As Wynter argues, when Christopher Columbus named the Americas and deemed them "for us," the "us" simultaneously identified those who were human and those whose humanity was immediately put into question and would remain in question: Native peoples, including those from the global

South. These distinctions began in the realm of the church, determining who were holier religious subjects, and then moved into the realm of the state, determining who were better subjects of the state. Schooling, either through the church or the state, plays a key role in managing, rewarding, and punishing colonial subjects, also known, in more human terms, as teachers and students, as those who know and those who learn.

The distinctions of who can be a teacher and who must be a learner is in keeping with coloniality as a pervasive thematic ordering of people for the purposes of domination and subjugation. Coloniality enacts this ordering through policies, laws, cultural practices, and knowledge production, all of which permeate access to material needs like potable water. The codification of laws favors the interests of those deemed human, and interpersonal interactions that echo these concentrations of power and related concentrations of suffering. Settler colonialism seeks to enact strata for the purpose of property accumulation for the few. Rather than establishing relationships to land in which it is treated as ancestor, source of life, teacher, and living, agentic entity, as is often manifested in Indigenous knowledge systems, settler colonialism seeks to establish and justify invasive and extractive relationships to land through the logic of property. In the way that property and progress are conflated in Gast's painting, so are these things conflated in problematic relationships in higher education. And yet, as the work of public intellectuals like Leilani Sabzalian shows, there has never been a ceding of ancestral histories and knowledge systems to the stories that coloniality has told us. Rather than using *The Oregon Trail* as a neutral computer game in elementary curriculum, Sabzalian and her colleagues situated it as a malignant fiction and way to reclaim the central place of Indigenous knowledge systems for children.[18]

When Dulani hesitated to tell a story of herself in her college application essay, she was tapping into a complex mix of gift economies, feelings of indebtedness, and what is known as "stereotype threat," a term coined by social psychologists Claude Steele and Joshua Aronson in the 1990s. "Stereotype threat" conveys the lower level of performance that Black American teenagers measure in themselves when taking a standardized test in the company of white American students.[19] They both researched and intervened on the phenomenon that "when the allegations of the stereotype are importantly negative, this predicament may be self-threatening enough to have disruptive effects of its own." In other words, seeing oneself through the lens of a discriminatory society will damage a minoritized person's ability to succeed in time-sensitive, high-stakes tests. In later research, Steele found that telling female students that their gender wasn't a predictive factor of their test scores interrupted patriarchy's steady message that women should be smaller—in intellect, in the volume of their voice, and in physical terms. Yet, Dulani wasn't only seeing herself as part of a projected lower intellect: she was apprehensive of what implicit agreement she was entering into with a predominantly white institution. How many other times might she be asked to tell her "story"? If she were to continue with her established success as a learner and student, to whom might those accomplishments be attributed, such as the university's diversity initiatives? These are all cautions that Dulani expressed to me over years, cautions that she and I discussed as members of different generations that shared some of the pitfalls of initiatives fixated on diversity optics.

Independent scholar and public intellectual Sara Ahmed has discussed the gift economy as it entangles higher education's diversity initiatives. In her book *On Being Included*, she focuses specifically on the people tasked with being "diversity workers."[20] These positions might include academic diversity and equity associate deans in specific units of a university, or chief diversity officers in the top levels of administration. Their range of duties can include everything from being responsible for a university's attempts to diversify its students, staff, and faculty to being the office where students go when they have experienced harm in the classroom or on campus. These positions have experienced dramatic growth since the early 2000s. According to modest estimates, two-thirds of universities have senior administrative diversity positions. The demand has been so great it has yielded cottage industry search firms whose sole focus is the recruitment and hiring of diversity officers—for a fee, of course. From diversity officers that are funded through the year-to-year whims of a central office, to admissions processes that are governed by a white professoriate, students, faculty, staff, and students of color can easily understand themselves to be the recipients of someone else's benevolence in higher education. In Ahmed's study, one researcher names the debt bind, and Ahmed sums up the power relationship:

> Our diversity team experienced the consequences of being a tick in the box. We embody diversity for the organization not only because our research project was on diversity but because we were legible as a sign of diversity (a team of many colors). We were continually reminded that we were the recipients of generous funding. We were indebted. The gift economy is powerful: a means of some asserting the power they have given to others, which is at once a power to expect or demand a return. Diversity becomes debt.

These problematic power relations are challenging to even speak out loud, in part because the cacophony of diversity and inclusion are so predominant that it is difficult to stop and ask, what do we mean by diversity or inclusion? Moreover, these relationships to "being diverse" are difficult to interrogate or rewrite because pursing diversity becomes the work, rather than interrupting systemic oppression. Ahmed explains that when uttered, "racism is treated as a breach in the happy image of diversity." She also succinctly captures the quintessential bind in which people—yes, even tenured faculty—name racism and other vectors of oppression as living problems on campuses, but then become the problem to be excised. Manifest destiny long ago provided the narrative that those who carry out conquest do so as a moral, even divine, imperative. Not so distant from this idea is that those who bequeath admission, scholarship, and credentials do so out of munificence. Encoded in that munificence is the power to surveil and trim away from articulations of power, including funding, that sully the optics of diversity. People are made to be in debt to their university through the mechanisms of tuition, loans, and temporary contracts. In this delimited capitalist calculus, the dehumanizing goal is to move from being in debt to being a creditor. As Black studies scholar Cedric Robinson and the nation's first sociologist, W. E. B. Du Bois both argued, capitalism cannot function without racism. Social geographer and activist Ruth Wilson Gilmore put it succinctly: "Capitalism refines stratification of well-being, and racism enshrines it."[21] Racial capitalism is a crucial concept for contending with universities, and settler colonialism as a societal structure provides further tools for reckoning with multiple forms of oppressions that rely on each other.

INTERLOCKING PIECES
OF A RUNNING SETTLER ENGINE

Rather than a single event or a long-gone historical era, settler colonialism is a continuous process and structure that hinges on three mutually dependent practices, all of which work in tandem, relying on each other to maintain cohesion.[22] The first practice is the seizure of the land, resources, cultural practices, and goods of a desired location. Beginning with land grabs in the fourteenth century and continuing through contemporary times, the United States was founded on the practice of outsiders claiming land and resources. Historian Roxanne Dunbar-Ortiz describes the United States as a culture of conquest that facilitates property quests at all costs.[23] Within the structure of settler colonialism, there can never be enough land to satisfy the thirst of a few. Today, echoes of the invasions of Native land and opportunistic treaties with Native peoples are evident in the private takeover of public, potentially collective spaces as well as the trend of turning universities into corporate entities.[24] There was a time when college didn't automatically conjure the word "debt," but that time is over. Settler colonialism and its interests of profit and property have a great deal to do with why debt has materially shaped what college means, even though the narratives of "college for all" rarely name these realities.[25] As the Gast painting's prominence in history textbooks so poignantly articulates, the consequences of college debt and who profits from it means rewards for some and obstacles for many more.

This logic is also present in the land grabs of K–12 public schooling spaces that have quickly blurred the lines between public monies and private ownership. As one pervasive example, charter schools began as an education policy whose intent was to foster the creation of culturally specific and culturally responsive schools to children and families who are largely disserved by a traditional Eurocentric curriculum. Charter schools such as the Indigenous-focused Old Main STREAM Academy mentioned in the author's note, as well as the Folk Arts–Cultural Treasures School in Philadelphia, are reflections of this intent. However, far more prominent are larger charter endeavors that have multiple locations, chief operating officers, and strict uniform and behavior codes for their students. As a result of the loosening of original charter plans, most charter schools are able to claim higher achievement rates because, unlike public schools, they are not obligated to accept and instruct children with specific special needs or children who are emergent bilinguals. In New Orleans, one of the nation's most treasured and simultaneously exploited Black cities, Hurricane Katrina created a havoc that literally swept away public education. Since Katrina's landfall in 2004 to the time of this writing, there has been a consistent erosion of public schools and teacher unions, to the point that only private and charter schools now remain. Many argue that charter schools are public schools, in that they receive funding through the same conduits, but they are not subject to the same regulations for accepting all students in their geographic zone. As a result, it is not unusual to see many young Black people in New Orleans not in classrooms during school hours. They have been cast out of their own domain: public schools in their neighborhoods. New Orleans is also, consequentially, home to some of the most profound youth-led movements for freedom, such as the Rethink nonprofit that prioritizes youth leadership through political education.

The erasures of neighborhoods and schooling are often facilitated—that is to say *justified*—by messages of assimilation and upward social mobility. The pressure that Dulani felt to act on behalf of her parents and not her own concerns and those of her peers illuminates what is often erased through the pursuit of raising oneself up through imaginary bootstraps. Neoliberal aims of multiculturalism are an infrared example of dispossession through representation.

While many campus protests have called for more diverse curricula in college courses, the ongoing hum of erasing to replace should caution all involved that ideas and knowledge long deemed as inherently objective will not be displaced easily or without objection. People in power have come into power by learning about objective research, even though all research is conducted by someone, in some place that has its own histories. While it is inarguable that a plural society requires diverse curricula, marking of some texts as "diverse" or "multicultural" runs the risk of labeling these texts as other, in which case Eurocentric texts, or whiteness more broadly, continue to represent the center. As many scholars of semantics have written, an entity is defined as not being the other entity. Whiteness is notoriously defined as not being Black, going back to the one-drop rule, which dictated that if there is one drop of African blood in your lineage, you are Black. Once, during a discussion of patriarchy in a doctoral class I was teaching, I asked what it meant to be recognized as a man. One brilliant student gave a succinct definition: "You prove you're a man by not being a woman." Hence, even while many women of color may hold positions with status, that does not necessarily mean that power relations have shifted.

The second component of settler colonialism is erasure of Indigeneity. For Native Americans, erasure remains an ongoing front of contestation with the US government and other institutions in the fields of law, education, and science. They must be eliminated in order for settlers to replace them, and to justify and sustain the fundamental mission of the settler land grab. State-sanctioned erasure occurs in conjunction with the practice of settler colonialism as a form of cultural conquest. As historian Patrick Wolfe put it, "This logic holds that indigenous peoples must disappear. In fact, they must *always* be disappearing, in order to enable non-indigenous peoples' rightful claim to land. Through this logic of genocide, non-Native peoples then become the rightful inheritors of all that was indigenous—land, resources, indigenous spirituality, and culture."[26] A key logic of settler colonialism is erasing to replace. The land grabs relied on and continue to rely on codified blood quantum laws to ensure the gradual diminishment of Native peoples and their ultimate replacement by settlers. In Gast's painting, settlers, covered wagons, and trains have replaced Native and Black Americans with an implicit idea of linear progress.

Returning to New Orleans, in 2017, four of that city's Confederate memorials—including larger-than-life statues of Confederate heroes such as Robert E. Lee—were removed by municipal order. This move was preceded by decades of protest and resistance to the presence of these statues, with the city's writers and artists providing music and poetry that communicated the experience of growing up in the shadow of these statues, as well as the much larger wisdom of their ancestors who found ways to love, live, and struggle joyfully. Still, it is possible to visit New Orleans as a tourist and never encounter the messages in that artistry or the political education groups that have persevered even when schools were shuttered. Similarly, the removal of statues and monikers of owners of enslaved peoples on campuses is essential, but does not necessarily displace the settler relationships that are woven through society and higher education. These statues and building names honoring deceased leaders who engaged in the practice of owning human beings are, without a doubt, harmful to the students who are descendants of enslaved peoples; however, their removal does not necessarily change power structures. In a town hall meeting with administrators and students at Princeton University in 2016, one young Black woman stated plainly: "I do not want to sit in Wilcox Hall and enjoy my meal while looking at Woodrow Wilson because he would not want me here. And you don't understand that as a white person."[27] She is undoubtedly correct that the prominent placement of this portrait of a racist eugenicist implicitly upholds whiteness as more important than addressing racism. Moreover, her observation that the apprehension of this reality is not readily available to everyone, even those who have matriculated to the highest ranks of academe, speaks loudly to the consequences of an education system that centers Euro-descendent men and their victories. Yet, were Wilson's portrait to be removed as an isolated act, when and how might students learn about the key, ongoing component of settler colonialism: stolen labor and anti-Black racism? When and how might the largely white administrative ranks of higher education understand how their ascendancy is relationally connected to the white imagination of a nation that structurally relied on this stolen labor? If only it were as simple to remove these honorifics.

Theft of labor is the third practice that settler colonialism relies on. It is founded on importing forced labor and attempting to render human beings as chattel. In this process, humanity is immediately subjugated as property. Enslaved African peoples were considered chattel long before the cargo ships reached their destinations, with the bodily treatment of the captured Africans standing as the first act in an ongoing process to strip away their humanity.[28] Continuing through the contemporary prison industrial complex and the pressure on migrants forced to accept low-wage labor, labor exploitation is necessary to harvest the resources of the land, and, through economic stratification and sequestering, ensure that land and property rights are reserved for a much smaller group of settlers.[29] The logic of property interests drives all institutions in settler societies to maximize profit for a few from the labor of many. While capitalism as an economic system also follows a logic of stratification and is a key structural aspect to the US, capitalism, as a theory or as a praxis, does not hold the same analytic force for understanding land in relation to life as settler colonialism does. Cedric Robinson's theorization of racist capitalism provides necessary, companion analytics for ascertaining the fundamental intertwining of racism and capitalism.[30] Situating learning and studying that involves tumult on college campuses necessitates situating higher education, literally, in relationship to land, racism, and capitalism in settler societies. From this stance, protests merge out of and are a reaction to this structure.

The establishment of higher education has been through the intertwined practices of settler colonialism. As Wilder put it, along with the church and state, higher education acts as the third pillar of this nation. It reflects and refreshes the interlocking practices of settler colonialism: land seizure, erasing to replace, and creating and relying on chattel labor.[31] The settler colonial project first constructed colleges as places for the ministerial education of wealthy men, with strict focus on Greek, Latin, geometry, logic, ethics, and theology.

With virtually no space for discussion or dialogue, the colleges favored what Freire termed in 1970 a "banking approach" to education, wherein students, even the privileged male students, were seen as vessels in which the culture of the colony should be sown, in essence advancing the project of knowledge for the purpose of domination and property accumulation.[32] As Wilder details in his analysis of the reliance and sustenance of slavery through elite institutions of higher education, private land-owning entities were integral to a slavery-based economy. Within the physical buildings on elite campuses, the knowledge systems created by and for society's most elite members, and the codification of research and knowledge, all worked to the benefit of those who were elevated by a slavery-based settler society: white, land-owning men. This held distinct yet deeply connected implications for other peoples. "Normal schools," as schools of education were previously known, were created for the circumscribed education of white women and to train them as teachers. At least until they married. This history of gender in education is both a mirror of and window into contemporary teacher education: it reflects and provides insight into the issues related to schoolteachers being predominantly white women. The teaching population is overwhelmingly white, female, and middle to middle-upper class. As gender studies scholars have brilliantly articulated, schools of education are animated by plantation politics that are feminized yet rarely feminist.[33]

Agitating these structures and patterns is a difficult, often uncomfortable lane to navigate. In my own experience as a teacher, I have heard and felt the subtle yet crystal-clear direction to get back into my lane of keeping students—who some even refer to as "clients"—happy rather than engaging them in the challenging yet necessary reckoning with historical facts and the flimsy idea that a well-intentioned teacher who enacts racism can still be exonerated because she has good intentions. In every course that I have taught in which racism and settler colonialism is in the curriculum, students fittingly experience different kinds discomfort. In essence, I ask them to use their understanding of critical race theory and settler colonialism to see the world differently. I ask a largely white student body to let go of the myth that colonization is a thing of the past, to understand how it pulses through our practices and policies. I ask them to be with themselves and the world not as saviors but as informed advocates, even co-conspirators. In short, I ask them to let go of the national lies they've been socialized to love. And I have seen them do it. I can clearly see the strain that accompanies deconstructing the lies they've learned to love and then reconstructing how they encounter themselves and society. It is deeply transformative and may take time well beyond a semester's end date to have some of the lies truly unraveled.

As one of my former students, a phenotypically white woman who is ethnically Latinx, told me: "It took me a long time to understand what you meant [about the creation of categories to deliver harm], but that sentence you said just stayed in my head." Race was created to deliver racism, and the category of race is too often seen as simple biological fact. Because categories, including race, gender, sexuality, and class, are ubiquitous, it can be easy to overlook that these categories are constructs with crushingly real material consequences. For example, Black and Native peoples experienced disproportional rates of infection and death from the COVID-19 pandemic. However, they were at risk not because of their race, but because of the social conditions, such as lack of access to healthcare or being paid low wages to stock shelves in stores that made them already vulnerable to a pandemic that hooked into existing inequities. As my former student told me, and as I have witnessed, it is neither a singular nor easy venture to detangle oppression from the categories created to deliver it.

Returning to the cultural texts that facilitate the lies that people come to love about this nation, white women have a particular place in settler colonialism. In addition to illustrating the linear, "natural" conquest of the frontier and the Western technologies used to conquer it, Gast's painting also teaches about white patriarchy. The painting depicts many white men, traveling, tilling land, and conducting trains, but they are all overwhelmingly dwarfed in comparison to a larger-than-life, floating image of the blond-haired white women and her flowing white dress. Like everyone in the painting, she is also looking westward. The image is far from subtle: one of purity, a woman worth conquering so-called wild lands for, a woman worth protecting. For the protection of white women, lynchings of Black men, accused only of looking or whistling at a white woman, have taken place as celebrations of white supremacy. Artist Ken Gonzales-Day's visual art series "Erased Lynchings" focuses on the postcards of photographed lynchings that were circulated during the Jim Crow era and beyond as mementos of a racist popular culture.[34] Gonzalez-Day's artistry lies in his erasing of the images of murdered victims from these lynchings, bringing into sharp focus the joy of the white spectators who gathered to celebrate the spectacle of anti-Black brutality.

While artists and activists have brought to the fore these grotesque realities of settler colonialism and racism, it is all too rare that education experts call out the glaring problem regarding the instruction of Indigenous, Black, and other children of color by white women who, largely, have been socialized to see these children through a deficit lens. Writer, scholar, and organizer Carla Shalaby so eloquently names this cultural and racial chasm as a societal problem in which unruly children are seen as troublemakers to be tamed, instead of the people who are crying for freedom the loudest in schools.[35] Within my own experience, the particular power dynamics held by white women who, through patriarchy, rarely access the highest realms of power, often violently reinforce racist and settler power relations as a way to enact power over others.[36] This takes the form of tone-policing women of color, having low expectations of them, and expressing disappointment in "diversity hires" behind the closed doors of promotion and tenure meetings. These patterns, although obviously not across the board, are substantive enough to eerily reflect what higher education scholar Elon Dancy refers to, among other racialized dynamics in universities, as "plantation politics."

The structure of settler colonialism reaches far beyond private institutions and their collusion with slavery-based political economies. The logic that Indigenous lands should be redistributed as settler state property is present in public institutions. As countless other have stated, there is no such thing as clean money, so it follows that there is such a thing as land that inertly awaits appropriation.

Land grant institutions were established in the United States in the mid-1800s. Pioneer land grant universities, as they were first known, focused on agriculture and engineering. The Morrill Acts, passed by Congress in 1862 and 1890, established these institutions—the "land" in their title referring less to the technological expertise they were meant to develop than to the large tracts of federal land reserved for them. The acts coincided with the Homestead Acts of the 1800s, which created homesteads out of Indigenous lands by federal decree, and then delineated how those homesteads should be apportioned to US citizens, deliberately excluding the sovereignty of Indigenous peoples and land.[37] Similarly, the Morrill Acts detailed how much federal land was to be set aside for these "public' institutions, furthering racialized educational opportunity in the agriculture and technological fields, and supporting the transition from a slave-based economy that marked the mid-1850s while still supporting whiteness as property. The second Morrill Act, passed in 1890, is commonly understood to be the congressional establishment of historically Black college and universities, or HBCUs, was in fact vociferously debated by elected officials, all white. Ultimately, the second Morrill Act did provide funding for Black people to enter higher education that had been restricted to white people. However, the provisions had constraints, in line with racial segregation. As historian Katherine Wheatle explains, it required states either "to prove that race was not a criterion for admission to the already established land-grant college, or establish, from its own revenue, a school of agriculture and industrial education for African Americans—particularly those residing in the South."[38] The debate and provisions of the second act created a contradictory set of terms for Black people's entrance into higher education, while excluding them from white institutions and, more pointedly, their resources.[39] Wheatle's examination is an important contribution to understanding how settler colonialism has worked within legal codes to negatively impact Black and Indigenous peoples simultaneously but through different processes. Property was deemed public by virtue of the federal government, but the vast majority of land under discussion and apportionment was and remains unceded Indigenous territory.

As an example of the strategic reach of the quest for delineating property rights, the Morrill Acts included provisions for states' rights to federal property when there wasn't sufficient federal property in a given state. Cornell University, despite its private status, was named as the land grant institution for the state of New York, but there were no further lands the state could decree to the University. Instead, as outlined in the Morrill Act, Cornell was apportioned timber from the state of Wisconsin.[40] The timber was not used for any construction purpose at Cornell, but was later sold for a profit that moved the university, then at risk of bankruptcy, into financial stability, greatly increasing its endowment and viability as an elite private institution. This cluster of claims and conversions of sovereign land into property is a vivid example of the logics of property and profit that have quite predictably circulated through the establishment and maintenance of universities in a settler colonial society.

The settler project of erasure is also found throughout many of the current and historical manifestations of higher education's curricula, a logic that founded Indian boarding schools in the philosophy encapsulated in the phrase "kill the Indian to save the man."[41] Contemporary manifestations of this logic include higher education's continued use of a banking approach with Eurocentric curricula. As Wilder points out in his historical analysis of the roles elite institutions of higher education played in supporting, exploiting, and perpetuating slavery in the US, research that fails to investigate the social positioning of those "cast on the underside of humanity" bolsters the stratification of society by normalizing the widely held belief that those with less can be assimilated into upper social strata. As a result, the cultural practices and knowledges of the upper strata are reified as inherently better.[42]

Higher education is, like other social fields in capitalist-anchored settler colonies, predicated on individuals holding differential status so that many are competing for the limited and protected well-being afforded to higher status, reflected in salary and reputation. And like the military and the Catholic church, higher education is a strictly hierarchal system. As mentioned before, it is largely only those who have attained the highest ranks of professor who weigh in on the promotion of more junior scholars. Within higher education, publication and grant procurement represent the forms of capital that translate most readily into higher status for professors.[43] However, how have those who received grants and published articles been socially positioned and privileged to do so?

Prior to any of that happening, students must be admitted. For a white upper-middle-class family, life after high school has almost always meant higher education, often free from debt. For a Black upper-middle-class family, postsecondary admission likely still includes a complex bundle of racial capitalist realities. These include but are not limited to the burden of debt, the implicit gates of respectability politics, and suspicions that they are students not because they are intelligent but because they are the recipients of "hand-outs." And dinner table talk in a wealthy home would likely entirely leapfrog over the issue of access to higher education, moving swiftly on to what career path and what schools might be suitable. It is common parlance in white upper-middle-class families to talk of "dream schools" and "safety schools," code for where "rising seniors" might apply for admission. This discussion may not even be necessary, as legacy admissions could already have been secured through the previous generations that matriculated at Ivy League schools. The youth in these families might even see themselves reflected through familial connections to campus building's names that reflect a sizable donation. At a minimum, these starkly different generational histories and relationships with higher education mean different prices and expectations for admission.

Although it happened many years ago, I distinctly recall a department-wide deliberation of doctoral applicants. We had spent many hours before this day-long meeting reading applicants' letters, their GRE scores, their GPAs, and I was early advised to observe not just the content of their letters of recommendation, but *who* had written the letters. In other words, what counted more than the content of the letter was the social capital of who these applicants knew. Already, the admissions deliberations were skewed toward those applicants who had the means to be in contact with high-profile scholars of education. As my colleagues and I came to our conclusion about our top ranking choices, we were interrupted by our department chair, begrudgingly telling us that one of the applicants who had not made our top "cut" was the daughter of a person who had donated a significant amount of money to the institution. The message was clear without being spoken: we were to admit this student and remove a different student from the admission pool.

By reflecting rather than interrupting hierarchies based on competition and status, the academy has sustained problematic relationships with vulnerabilized communities.[44] After the department's deliberation concluded, I contacted an alumna of our master's program to explain to her, a brilliant Black woman, that she had not been accepted. While I did not share the cringeworthy decision that led to the rejection of her application, neither did I tiptoe around the truth that this same institution that had partially subsidized her master's degree, opened up her horizons to see what a doctoral degree might mean for her and her education mission, had also denied her that path to a PhD. I'm delighted and unsurprised that this woman, drawing on the strength of her family and her belief in herself, pursued her doctoral degree from a well-regarded university.

Nevertheless, she is part of the vulnerabilized communities that universities are intricately tied to out of their need for research subjects, for grants to conduct research upon "at-risk" populations and to extend the gift of scholarships out of their munificence. In many academic meetings, collaborations with "the community" are discussed according to a notion that there is a singular community outside of the university or—perhaps an even more dangerous notion—that the academy itself is composed of a singular group of people similar in their shared ways of being, knowing, and doing, also known as culture.

There are several interlocking pieces of these settler logics and practices within higher education. Some of these patterns have transpired through scholarship that has worked from and validated racist premises of societal difference.[45] For example, recent frameworks such as those tracking individuals with grit or a growth mindset have been used to diagnose the problem within youth, often poor and Black, Indigenous, and/or of migrant families.[46] If they only had more grit, they would, purportedly, tough their way through intertwined obstacles such as discrimination in housing and employment, poorly resourced K–12 schools, environmental racism, and familial forced separation. Another common instantiation is the practice in which researchers seek access to communities to study them, publish about the problems therein, but the community members gain little to nothing in return and are rarely fairly compensated for their time as research participants.[47] I have heard the question "How do I gain access to communities?" from dozens of academics. As the child of migrants, I have often thought and sometimes asked, "Why should you have access?" The question itself speaks of a sense of entitlement, at least one of expectation.

As philosopher Jeremy Bentham articulated over his arc of writings, the mere expectation of property is an enactment of property rights. And this expectation does not arise from thin air. Universities, particularly research-intensive universities, communicate to their newly hired faculty that they must be researching and publishing early, often, and always. However, knowledge-making projects, also known as research projects, are fundamentally relational practices. The same is true of teaching and learning—they are fundamentally relational. Settler colonialism has curdled this relationship, so that even in collaborative research projects, academics are often cast as the researchers and teachers or other professionals are cast as practitioners. Paid academics are the ones who should have the prestige to display their expertise and, consequently, hold more material resources and symbolic power in knowledge relationships. Just as K–12 teachers perpetuate racism, heteropatriarchy, and ableism through their practices, higher education faculty do so in relation with their teaching and research. They also refresh the concept of whiteness as property.

As research within higher education and higher education itself tends toward a corporate model of commodification, these patterns manifest themselves into "selling" experiences, such as service learning. Service learning does not take place without people who are deemed to be in need of service. When grants are awarded for researchers and aspiring researchers to conduct service-learning projects, those grant monies inevitably run out. For example, a service-learning project may briefly provide a community with a literacy tutor but, just as the project ends, that community is left without a tutor while the researcher enjoys the benefit of writing about their findings. The tutors are likely to be students who come from some generational wealth and spend a majority of their time as a tutor either learning about the knowledge already in that community or reifying racialized ideas of what counts as "proper" English. A close friend and one of the most powerful teachers in my life put it succinctly: "Just because you can think of an interview question doesn't mean that you get to ask it." Access should begin with listening, waiting for invitations, and working alongside, rather than from above. Who is researched and who owns the literal data of a research project concertedly manifest settler colonial logics and practices.

And yet, there are myriad examples of academics who work to move material resources into the hands of people and neighborhoods that have been harmed by university extraction so that they can archive their own knowledge systems as they see fit. There are community-based panels that review any research proposals for what potential benefits and harms they could mean for that specific community.[48] These practices remind us that knowledge-building has never been the purview just of universities and their employees. Learning and knowledge are both bigger than that.

In 1963, James Baldwin wrote that "American history is longer, larger, more various, more beautiful, and more terrible than anything anyone has ever said about it." His prescient and sadly still relevant words were part of his essay "A Talk to Teachers," specifically K–12 teachers.[49] Surely, the ways that schoolchildren of various social locations learn about conquest, destiny, and progress is implicated in the nation's project of profit for some at the expense of others. Yet, higher education, rather than interrupting these patterns for the benefit of a collective, plural society, seems to double down on them. Higher education, in many ways, occupies an equally deep, if not deeper, more various, and more problematic reality about property, land, debt, theft, and profit. Narratives of diversity, social mobility, and generational progress function together to blur higher education's history and interests in property and profit.

CHAPTER THREE

PROFIT AND DEBT

"Diversity . . . allows the accumulation of organizational value."
—SARA AHMED, *On Being Included*[1]

"We went to the public hospital but it was private, but we went
through the door marked 'private' to the nurses' coffee room, and it
was public. We went to the public university but it was private, but
we went to the barber shop on campus and it was public. We went
into the hospital, into the university, into the library, into the park.
We were offered credit for our debt. We were granted citizenship.
We were given the credit of the state, the right to make private any
public gone bad. Good citizens can match credit and debt. They get
credit for knowing the difference, for knowing their place. Bad debt
leads to bad publics, publics unmatched, unconsolidated, unprofit-
able. We were made honorary citizens. We honored our debt to the
nation. We rated the service, scored the cleanliness, paid our fees."

—STEFANO HARNEY and FRED MOTEN, *The Undercommons*[2]

I graduated from college in 1992. While that is certainly a long
time ago in years, it is perhaps an even longer time when mea-
sured in the ways higher education has adapted and shapeshifted in
regard to diversity and social protest. In the early '90s, I was more
than content to find a home at the University of Nebraska, Lincoln.
Since I had come from a then largely homogenous, white Omaha,
the sheer size and expansiveness of this large state college, with en-
rollments hovering near twenty thousand students, felt like a large

door opening for me. I spent my time in the stacks of the immense library, a few unremarkable large lecture courses, and most Fridays in a small, scrappy print journalism program that taught me skills that I continue to hone. Like not writing a sentence as long as I just did.

I became involved in small projects of student affairs like campaigns for increasing student union representation within the university as well as larger, global movements like the protests against apartheid in South Africa. I watched *A Different World* religiously, and grew a fierce love for politically conscious hip-hop and a still fiercer love for R&B. I also listened to Tracy Chapman, whose music then and now regularly describes the daily living conditions and desires of people under the heel of oppression. However, I think much of her deep political commentary passed over my head in the late '80s and early '90s in favor of the undeniable intimacy of her craft. For example, in the song "Fast Car," Chapman touches on generational poverty, desire for companionship, alcoholism, family separation, and moments of joy—all in a single rhythmically inviting and spare song featuring her voice and musical talent. Only later would I come to understand her creative talent and her political analysis as inseparable.

There was certainly more racial, gender, sexual, and class diversity on that large campus than in much of my K–12 schooling, but it was still an overwhelmingly white school in terms of faculty, staff, and students. Although I was one of a handful of South Asian students, particularly in the humanities, I did not feel as scrutinized or oddly looked upon as I was in high school. Unlike Dulani and college students in the wake of protests in the 1960s, I went to college at a time when the optics of diversity weren't such a valuable commodity on campuses. I graduated from college with only $6,000 in student debt from that public university.

Today is a sea change from those days, particularly when it comes to how racialization is articulated through university mechanisms.

In 2009, a large-scale federal budget cut to public colleges became permanent, leading to skyrocketing tuitions to cover administrative bloat and enormous budgets for facilities built to sell a commodified student experience. The significantly profound presence of social protest and student mobilization for justice and equity on college campuses, private and public, has led to the creation of myriad diversity, equity, and inclusion offices, often higher in academic status than they've ever been. But as far as these positions being an engine for institutional change, that has yet to be seen. If we heed Ahmed's research and deep analysis, they likely will not alter the conditions on college campuses.

In 2015, the chorus to a Kendrick Lamar hit song, "We gon' be alright!," often served as anthem for the social protests against anti-Black racism. History and literature testify strongly to the profound truth that despite the unrelenting march of colonialism, Native, Black, and other peoples of color have found ways to live, love, dance, fall in and out of love—to be all right. This resistance has been met with the mass loss of life and harrowing abuse from the dominant culture, but as Lakota scholar Nick Estes conveys in the title of his 2019 book, *Our History Is the Future*, Indigenous resistance has long existed in tandem with domination and the accumulation of wealth. More profoundly, Indigenous knowledges have preceded and will outlast the project of settler colonialism. As Estes describes of his time among the Standing Rock community, made up of Indigenous peoples of many lands, "In the twilight hours, Water Protectors told stories and shared the prophetic visions for a better world, not just in the past, but one currently in the making, as purple-grey smoke filled the spaces between tipis, tents, and lines of cars and trucks."[3]

Despite Estes's clarifying description of generational knowledge that grounds Indigenous longevity, resistance is not always so palpable, particularly on higher education campuses, where the student population's commitment is, by design, a short-term one. While protests continue to happen, particularly around isolated racist events, there is also the steady, trundling machinery of wealth accumulation. At the same time as bachelor's degrees have become more required for many entry-level positions, universities have increasingly turned to corporate models to build profit, meaning growth in high-tech buildings, more highly paid administrators, and rising tuition rates.[4] According to the Department of Education, between 1990 and 2010, enrollment in for-profit universities increased by 600 percent. Much of this growth then collapsed with the folding of several well-known entities, such as the ITT Technical Institute, but in the wake of that collapse, public and private colleges have steadily increased tuition rates, reduced students' benefits, and hired private marketing firms to help them bolster their branding to expand the economic base of student enrollment and increase student spending on campuses.[5] When I began my undergraduate degree, in 1988, some of the first pieces of mail I received were applications for credit cards with high interest rates. That practice has not changed. College and K–12 students face significant structural challenges if they do not come with the safety nets that white families with generational wealth provide.

In Gordian-knot fashion, rising tuition rates and fast-track training programs such as Teach for America have shaken higher education's economic base, in this case in the field of education. Founded by Wendy Kopp, Teach for America was outlined in her senior thesis at Princeton University. Kopp theorized that if students from the nation's top universities committed to teaching two years in under-resourced schools, then they would, upon their return to more monied and powerful positions, enact social change. In reality, Teach for America has imposed temporary teachers—who go through only a few weeks of training—upon thousands of Black and brown children in neighborhoods already enclosed and subject to environmental racism. It reflects a naïve standpoint that a typical English major, with scant teacher training, could be an effective teacher in a context they know nothing about. These young, majority-white teachers spend two years teaching children in working poor Black and brown neighborhoods end up only dabbling in the lives of children and families before they abruptly leave. Moreover, this fast-track program to becoming a teacher has been replicated into many other approaches to teacher certification. In reaction, higher education institutions scrambling for monies they could once count on through teacher education programs have sought solutions through capital investment campaigns, the marketing of a student campus experience, and moving rigorous professional development into online programs that can be completed quickly.[6]

When the COVID-19 pandemic started surging through the United States, campuses largely went all online in March 2020. That summer, not long after many university officials had written public statements denouncing the anti-Black racism that led to the killing of George Floyd, the result of a choking lasting eight minutes, forty-six seconds, campuses reopened. Many universities, including the University of North Carolina at Chapel Hill and Notre Dame, returned to all-online course delivery just weeks after students had arrived to campus in August, and rates of virus infection surged. The universities, particularly public institutions, chose to reopen because they had been in dire financial straits since the 2009 budget cuts. Out of financial desperation, universities sold a student experience, including housing and culinary options, while they simultaneously paid less attention to students' quality of learning.[7] More simply put, they were seeking to follow the business model of the typical movie theater, in which more revenue comes from the popcorn and soda than movie ticket sales. This comparison helps to explain why more monied institutions, like Boston College, with its $2.5 billion endowment, chose to reopen its campus to in-person classes along with some online options during the ongoing months of the pandemic through 2020. It had long run on a business model bent on maximizing profit. Without a captive consumer base of students paying for lodging in residence halls and purchasing food in dining halls, universities faced a revenue shortfall. Even those universities who economically could have weathered this setback chose not to, out of an interest to maintain the size of the endowment. Universities that have learned to act like banks have no interest in losing money.

Settler colonialism desires wealth and property for a few, but that cannot happen without the displacement and debt of millions. Debt is intimately tied to wealth. In fact, in this capitalist society, the very structure of economic stratification dictates that many must constitute an underclass, meaning they are housing and food insecure, so that a few may profit greatly. This is the foundation of capitalism, more specifically racial capitalism, in which racism and class stratification intersect to reproduce race and class stratification across generations. Even Marxist critiques of capitalism have been susceptible to the clutches of Eurocentric thought. As the late Black studies scholar Cedric Robinson eloquently wrote, "Marxism is a Western construction—a conceptualization of human affairs and historical development that is emergent from the historical experiences of European peoples mediated, in turn, through their civilization, their social orders, and their cultures."[8] The reopening of campuses in a global pandemic illustrates Robison's point, if we examine the rates of infection and deaths in college towns. In Pittsburgh, once a steel town and now a city fueled by the industries of higher education and healthcare, the rates of infection and death rose, but disproportionately. The University of Pittsburgh, a predominantly white school, reported, at the most, only six dozen active cases of the virus in one week on campus during the fall 2020 semester, but Black people in Pittsburgh were 3.3 times as likely to die from the virus than young white undergraduates. For colleges to reopen in cities like Pittsburgh, hourly paid jobs such as those for transportation workers and campus staff have to be in place. The racial trade-off between maintaining one group's safety at the expense of another is a common one, in which Black people die at higher rates because of environmental racism, working conditions, and lack of access to healthcare, even in a city whose tallest buildings are lit up with the names of medical centers.

Against the long-running history and present of racist capitalism, my memories and analysis of college in the early 1990s are not meant, in any way, to suggest it was better back then. While the country was dragging itself out from the punishing and public plundering of the Reagan administration, it was dealing with the burgeoning business of incarceration, the ramping up of convictions through President Bill Clinton's three-strikes policy, and a drug epidemic that was racialized to criminalize poor Black people. Up close, each of these actions may seem to have a unique logic and purpose. But, from a few steps back, just as with the classic metaphor of the canary's cage, what becomes visible is the overarching structure across the proliferation of places to contain and enclose human beings for profit. It preys upon society's canaries—the poor, queer, dis/abled people of color in order to create the appearance of a stream of money and jobs. Ruth Wilson Gilmore's exhaustive 2007 book, *Golden Gulag*, details how the prison industrial complex is not just about prison; it is an entire economic system and a shared ideology that people can be thrown away. Society hinged itself to the idea that enclosure and incapacitation are both moral and possible, building prison after prison after prison. Not coincidentally, projects of profit and domination are knitted into this mentality of surveillance and containment. In numerous instances, self-deputized white people have shot and killed Black people, with Trayvon Martin standing out in public memory of a life cut short by a self-appointed neighborhood watchperson because Martin was Black, young, and wearing a hoodie. Many have debated that George Zimmerman, the person who murdered Trayvon Martin, was of Latinx descent, so was this whiteness? As detailed in chapter 2 and below, whiteness as property does not only reside within bodies that are phenotypically white. At its core is the idea that, for someone like Zimmerman, surveillance and punishment were his to mete out. Gilmore's work, along with the work of other abolition scholar activists including Erica Meiners and Sabina Vaught, makes transparent how thoroughly incarceration exists as a material structure but even more dangerously as a population-level mindset. Meiners has researched and theorized the ways that universities participate in incarceration through explicit investment in carceral corporations as well as policies that do not admit undocumented migrants.

As is the pattern with so much of struggle and study, these scholars also detail how much knowledge creation happens within places of enclosure. All of them have, in different ways, been involved with study and action groups inside incarceration facilities and with people whose loved ones are incarcerated. Gilmore, Vaught, and Meiners also address the particular relationship they have when studying with and alongside people who are incarcerated, lifting up both a refreshing transparency about the purview of researchers and calling on researchers to be more responsible in studying, not from a place of high status but to study alongside and for those who likely won't write about their experiences in an academic journal. In a now-classic article that reframes the school-to-prison pipeline as the school-prison nexus, Meiners opens with a description of a conversation she had with an incarcerated man who asked why she was in the facility so frequently. Meiners explained her project of studying to interrupt carcerality. This incarcerated man replied, "Oh, so you study what I live?"[9] This sobering interaction reframes the kind of relationship that study and struggle can form. The dissonance itself allows for creating ways of being in relation that disrupt who knows and who is merely to be studied, and for what purpose. The field of education is obligated to reckon with its own carceral practices of containment and disposability, also known as detention and expulsion.

LAYING THE FOUNDATION

In 1993, law professor Cheryl Harris wrote what has become a landmark article, entitled "Whiteness as Property."[10] Her legal argument lays out in plain, well-supported detail how pervasive the project of whiteness is, and how it is intertwined with property and wealth. Harris opens by describing the ways that her light-skinned grandmother and other Black people often passed as white in order to work, to survive with perhaps just a few more coins in their pocket. Those sparse coins were small comfort for the sharp psychic trade-off that came with silently capitulating, in those working hours, to the act of passing for white so that it might help a family to live. Harris's poignant introduction provides the groundwork upon which she details how the legal system has moved the line of race to preserve whiteness as property throughout history, to make it durable and so ubiquitous that it is hardly even noticed.

Harris's analysis spans laws from the founding of the colonies through the 1990s that were codified to solidify de jure and de facto definitions of whiteness through the separation and subordination of Black and other peoples of color. For example, Harris explains how in the earliest laws, racialization of Black peoples and Indigenous peoples differed in categories, rights, and naming, but both sets of edicts undergirded whiteness as a form of property, starting with the right to claim others as property. Harris goes on to explain how the formation of white racial identity relied deeply on changing legal designations of Black peoples—first as property, then "part human," then a de jure but not de facto form of freedom. Across the various legal manifestations, Harris's analysis lays bare that the aim was clear—protect whiteness as a form of property rights, extending into the expectation of entitlement as itself a form of property rights.

The examples of white entitlement to wealth, including the cultural capital from some institutions of higher education, are ubiquitous. Two times, the US Supreme Court heard arguments from Abigail Fisher, who sued the University of Texas Board of Regents, alleging that she had been denied admission because she was white, and affirmative action for students of color had verily blocked her perceived entitlement. It didn't seem to matter that her final grade point average did not meet UT's minimum standard for in-state applications, nor the fact that the primary beneficiaries of affirmative action have been white women, more so than Black, Indigenous, Latinx, or Asian peoples.[11] As a case in point of Harris's argument of property taking the expectation of entitlement, Fisher's case went to the highest court in the land, based on the expectation of and entitlement to that form of whiteness. The Supreme Court ruled 4–3 against Fisher's case, upholding the race-conscious admissions policy of the school's regents.

As has been the case since affirmative action was first introduced, though, the question of who should benefit and has ironically benefited from it has been wildly debated and often trafficked in pan-ethnic categories that obscure a grasp of structural racism. In the late 2010s, conservative coalitions of Asian Americans built support to challenge admissions at various institutions, most notably Harvard University, claiming that affirmative action and race-conscious policies discriminated against Asian students.[12] In this complicated web of widely different experiences all mashed into the category of Asian, students of Asian descent have been colloquially known as the model minority, which works to uphold anti-Black racism through a not-so-subtle indictment of Black peoples in comparison to, in reality, a distinct population of Asian students' social class. The comparison, however fictive, fits easily in the national narrative of immigrant-bootstrap determination that taps into racism to justify who is admitted to universities. This is an extrapolation of one of Harris's key points: that race and property shapeshift to maintain property as a form of protection, in this case protection coming through obtaining credentials from more prestigious institutions. Harris's invaluable argument stands intact, as it rightly maintains a focus on how humanness and Blackness have been codified to be separate and always subject to question through the laws and cultural practices of the United States. To more fully understand property, though, the Indigenous concept of land as life as well as ancestral relation provides perspective that when the pursuit of property is central, we lose the fact that all life is intertwined.

Much of the settler colonial societal structure is focused on the need to erase Native peoples and replace them with settlers who related to land in terms of ownership, as well as owning multiple other forms of property, including people who were considered chattel slaves. Paradoxically, while the one drop rule meant that one drop of Black heritage in a person's blood legally cast a person to be less than human, blood quantum laws sought to progressively reduce the amount of Indigeneity in people. In other words, settler colonialism needed *more* Blackness in the form of chattel property to accumulate wealth, but less Indigeneity to rationalize the core project of creating and protecting property through containment and erasure. Without this pursuit of land as property, tied deeply to whiteness as property, the subsequent wealth accumulation projects of prison labor exploitation, private detention centers, and municipal codes that rapidly compound fees for petty crimes—to name just a few of the most visible aspects of containment—might well not have existed. Poverty and debt do not simply exist naturally. They are created and perpetuated on purpose. Wealth and property accumulation are tied to debt and enclosure. One cannot exist without the other. Because the institutions of higher education share the same settler colonial DNA, it is predictable (but not ethical) that higher education would also reflect and enact these ties between debt and wealth.

In March of 2019, headlines around the United States reflected shock at the FBI's indictments of several wealthy families, including two entertainment celebrities, who bribed high-profile institutions in exchange for their children's admission to higher education. Over fifty people were charged with fraud and bribery, many of whom were connected to the Edge College & Career Network, also known as The Key. Although The Key was founded in 2007, its core founder, William Singer, launched his first high-cost college counseling business in 1992.[13] Beyond this single trajectory, though, it's important to note that admissions to elite colleges have long entailed various routes that are based on factors far afield of merit or talent, including sizable donations by relatives that swing admissions decisions, legacy admissions, and the recruitment of college athletes whose talents accrue profit for colleges but who are not compensated beyond their cost of attendance.

The 2019 admissions scandals only proved to peel back the cover of what has been an ongoing intertwining of wealth and higher education. In some cases, wealthy parents paid Key hundreds of thousands of dollars, some in the millions, to create a gilded pathway for their children into elite universities, including Yale, the University of Southern California, and the University of Texas at Austin. Lawyers, hedge fund managers, college coaches, celebrities, and lawyers were charged for bribery. Coaches and testing company managers, including those affiliated with the College Board, were charged with accepting bribes in exchange for the manipulation of tests and for colluding with admissions officers and university administrators on behalf of these wealthy families. One of the most titillating examples is that of actress Lori Loughlin's daughters being recruited, subsequent to Loughlin's payment, to USC's crew team. There is no crew team at USC. Time will tell which charges lead to actual trials, and what sentences are subsequently handed down.

Compare this college admissions scandal with lesser-known cases of "educational fraud," and we'll see how racialization is used to bestow and deny property. While celebrities like Lori Loughlin were paying hundreds of thousands of dollars to ensure their children were accepted to an elite university, several Black mothers, all working-class, have been charged with crimes related to getting children into better public schools. In 2012, Tanya McDowell, who was homeless at the time, was sentenced to five years in prison for first-degree larceny. The court found her guilty of falsifying documents so that her six-year-old could attend school in Norwalk, Connecticut. McDowell was sentenced, in the same trial, for involvement in misdemeanor drug sales, but the falsification of her home address was classified as felony larceny. In 2017, Kelley Williams-Bolar was sentenced to three years in prison and ordered to pay $30,000 in restitution after using her father's address so that her children could attend public school in a better-resourced neighborhood. Williams-Bolar said, at the time, that she made the decision to seek a better education for her children after a brick smashed one of the windows in their home in Akron, Ohio. One school administrator in the neighboring and wealthier Copley-Fairlawn school district said, "Those dollars need to stay home with our students."[14] This public school leader was implying that Williams-Bolar, in essence, stole money from the students who were zoned to attend that school. In the tradition of political education study groups and freedom schools, education is a public good, one that belongs to and should serve all. Following the money of formal schooling, though, reveals a more complicated and racial capitalist reality.

Public K–12 schooling is funded via property taxes, which means that already racially segregated neighborhood schools receive fewer resources because of lower home values and rates of home ownership.

Wealthier, white neighborhoods have better resources for their public schools, and often parents whose careers afford them the ability to fundraise for the school. This reality exists not because of personal housing preferences but due to Jim Crow federal policies that then became de facto real estate practices that functionally drew a line around Black neighborhoods. Building from the fact that enslaved peoples could not own anything that they labored for, including the right to parent their children, redlining and other policies have made anti-Black racism pervasive throughout education for the descendants of enslaved peoples. Any Native child who has grown up on a reservation can explain enclosure. Without a knowledge of these policies, though, people practice a naïve and dangerous calculus of race as biological determinant of vulnerability.

The college admissions scandal, as it came to be called, is perfectly in line with the logic that the poor deserve less because they are poor, and the wealthy or even moderately well-to-do families deserve more because they have pulled themselves up by their bootstraps. This hologram of meritocracy cannot remotely account for the chasms in lived experiences. When we step back to consider how much more expensive and time-consuming it is to be poor than rich, then property preservation for a few comes into sharper focus as both a mirror of society and window into its fallacies.

The pattern is clear. A majority of people have intimacy with debt, enclosure, risk, and financial insecurity, and when the wealthy few are confronted about their entitlement, their response is shock, indignation, and apologies that speak of good intentions but do not address impact. The most elite schools in the nation were built through enslaved Black labor so that white, land-owning men could attend. Craig Steven Wilder's book *Ebony and Ivy* provides a careful history of the timelines, amounts of profit garnered, and the ongoing cost to humanity resulting from the construction, through slave labor, of the nation's Ivy League. Wilder draws the important connection that "the modern slave trade pulled peoples throughout the Atlantic world into each other's lives."[15] While it is true that we are all interconnected, Wilder poignantly points out that these relations can and have been harmful through plunder that traversed lands and oceans. Higher education's most elite schools were formed out of this relationship of enslavement and ownership, and therefore it stood beside church and state as the third pillar of a civilization built on bondage. Enslaved peoples obviously gained nothing from their labor and were subject to all the degradations that came with being viewed as property, while wealthy people—at that time, solely white men—accumulated property and credentials that also acted as a form of property. The reckoning with this history has barely begun, and it has proven to be one that reveals the harm to white people through their relationship to protecting domination.

In 2017, Georgetown University, a private Jesuit institution, made public its history of owning and selling, in 1838, 227 enslaved Black peoples as a financial strategy to protect the university's tottering wealth. A *New York Times* article about this history posed the poignant question: What does Georgetown owe the descendants of those enslaved peoples? It is a question that should rankle and agitate the very foundation of how the nation was formed through the ongoing erasure of Indigenous peoples and the containment and disposability of Black and brown peoples. Tellingly, accompanying the question of what is owed is the story of the founders of Georgetown, a group of Jesuit priests who overlooked their own theologically radical principles as they actively carried out the practice of owning other human beings. Education researcher and historian Joyce King has referred to the attenuation of humanity that comes with dominating other people and attempting to destroy their humanity, including their ways of knowing.[16] King refers to the consequences of epistemic nihilation, or, as one young person paraphrased at her request, the "zombification" that "also imprisons Whites in an ethically incapacitated state of dysconscious racism." They are trapped in a habit of mind that impairs people in the dominant culture to ascertain and apprehend the structural forces of oppression.

However, reckoning with dysconscious racism and the annihilation of knowledge systems is typically withheld in favor of the less precise and therefore weaker notion of implicit bias. Myriad professional development sessions for educators consist of workshops with the aim of articulating and reducing implicit bias. These trainings confirm that growing up in a racialized society will lead to implicit biases. Ironically, the implicit message is this: we all have biases, which creates a false equivalency between different kinds of bigotry. But King pushes us to think more deeply about what it means to a person's humanity to not be able to see, to apprehend, to understand the intertwined structures that recreate anti-Black racism across generations. Focusing on implicit bias makes it easy to have conversations about peoples' experiences and not touch on structures that create material reality. Dysconscious racism forces us to reckon with an ethical collapse that comes with not being able to comprehend systemic oppression precisely because you benefit from it.

The United States operates on meritocracy, where hard work, being a good person, and playing by the rules will open up doors to security and upward social mobility. The stark examples of the college admissions scandal and the criminalization of Black parents not only shatter this myth but also demonstrate the punishments and debts that are levied against those who do not have access to easeful pathways for success, let alone wealth.

IN THE EVERYDAY
Property accumulation and debt is ubiquitous in higher education; it happens every day on college campuses, without any headlines or news crews documenting it. As Cheryl Harris observed, the idea of whiteness as property is so normalized, we hardly notice it.

It is a well-known fact that faculty of color on historically white campuses spend a disproportionate amount of time counseling students of color who have been subject to heteropatriarchy, transphobia, ableism, and classism, often in front of their peers in classrooms. Ironically, most diversity workers, as Sara Ahmed noted, are neither funded nor given institutional power to make structural or cultural changes. They are, in essence, asked to be cul-de-sacs where stories of harm are heard but not empowered by the institution to address formally. This pattern is itself a way of obscuring structural oppression that is perpetuated through whose knowledges and experiences are valued, and whose are more regularly challenged.

Female professors of color are regularly called "Miss" or by their first names while, even in the same email, male professors are referred to as Dr. and their last name. It is these same women of color who students turn to for advice, solace, or a literal break from the ubiquity of whiteness. In their now-classic volume *This Bridge Called My Back*, scholar feminists Cherríe Moraga and Gloria Anzaldúa compiled *testimonios*, firsthand research offerings, all from woman of color, that detail the ways that BIPOC female professors are asked to carry, on their spiritual, physical, and intellectual backs the weight of a racist, patriarchal, ableist, homo- and transphobic structure. Moreover, they are asked to bear witness. Bearing witness is a long and important aspect of specifically Black cultures, meaning more than simply observing. It means to join with, to lock arms, to support, and to be in a collective.[17]

When students seek out these professors, they often do so out of a need to speak out loud the structural weight that is bearing down upon them. They speak of having to leave a large part of their identity outside the classroom, as the curricula and the pedagogy communicate to them that their histories do not count. As one specific example, students with hidden disabilities are tasked with approaching their professors, many of whom may have had no education about the fact that abilities are always dynamic in nature. While a disability, documented or not, points to a set of needs, those needs are neither fixed nor static; they are in flux with the design, pace, and tone of a task or class. The student is the one who must begin the conversation, in which they also likely have to educate their professor about the dynamic nature of their needs. Even with these efforts, professors who have been socialized, and rewarded, for providing pre-determined content and not regarding learning as a relational activity, often are out of compliance with the accommodations that documented disabilities should be afforded. On rare occasions, allegations of noncompliance are brought to administrators' attention, often by faculty of color, and then often the incidents are handled by a meeting, typically ending in assigning a different advisor or instructor to the student.

The complex labor of raising an issue to a person in power, of listening to students and advocating for them, often collapses into the equivalent of finding a detour on a road in need of repair. In higher education, though, that road of white male privilege is rarely seen to be in need of repair. While students who do not reflect the mythic typical student and BIPOC faculty gather to listen, make plans, and advocate, white professors who have harmed students continue to write articles and pay, in terms of time and labor, certainly nothing close to restitution. Their cultural capital increases through publications, which results in grants, awards, promotions, and salary increases. Sometimes, they publicly admit their lack of knowledge, but again, this kind of statement far from meaningfully addresses the impact through efforts that address the structure and culture of higher education. Practices that do not collapse structure into personality conflicts would include reconsidering the processes in place to hire and retain faculty, how dis/ability, in this example, itself can be understood as the reality of being human rather than being aberrant from a mythic norm. Put another way, redressing systemic harm must involve addressing systems that recreate categories of normal and deviant.

Instead of the all-too-common request that people who have experienced oppression create 'honey-do lists," as Eve Tuck puts it, people who have benefited from the structure must stop investing in that structure.[18] They can and should find and participate in long-standing anti-oppression organizations, read a lot, and speak less. They should do the work of tracing critical genealogies of knowledge systems that have, frequently, been homogenized and recast through Eurocentric frames. When people who have harmed seek mea culpas in public without having done that work, it is another example of what Moraga and Anzaldúa refer to as "this bridge called my back." In this case, it is the burden of having an apology forced upon them that functions more like a request for absolution. Seeking absolution benefits them and does precious little to alter settler structures.

Beyond the publicized instances of wrongdoing, such as Georgetown's history of profiting from enslavement, the interlocking nature of racism and heteropatriarchy pervades everyday life in this settler colony. They are literally woven into required practices in universities and in structures, including gendered family roles. Women regularly receive lower quantitative scores on course evaluations, which, again, negatively affects their chances for promotion, tenure, research grants, and awards.[19] Often identified as gender bias, this phenomenon is more accurately referred to as heteropatriarchy, a system that works across institutions to benefit men, especially those who are perceived to be heterosexual. During the COVID-19 pandemic months in the spring and summer of 2020, a study observed that submissions of research articles by women dropped significantly, with the study's authors noting that the responsibilities of parenting and the labor of homemaking still disproportionately relied on women.[20]

Rather than tackle the fact that the highest course evaluations go to white professors, regardless of discipline or teaching approach, and that this demographic makes up 84 percent of full-time professors, mentors and teaching workshops are offered to junior faculty of color under the idea that if they only had better mentoring or self-organization skills, the demographics of the most powerful in higher education would change. In recent years, organizations like the National Center for Faculty Development and Diversity, which focuses on supporting diversity in higher education, have been highly sought after by both individual faculty and institutions. Members—meaning faculty of color—receive regular emails every Monday with tips on how to manage their time, delegate duties—in essence self-help their way through a hierarchical system. Thousands of faculty have found these tips useful for navigating the university, but the fact remains that only 2.2 percent of all full professors in the United States are Black women. The implicit idea of these coaching tactics is that by improving professors' teaching and time management strategies, the ranks of full professor will open themselves up easily to people of color. Again, the myth of meritocracy looms large, woven with individualism: if you acted better, organized yourself better, you will be rewarded.

Yet, the property and profit reserved for a few stays intact through the widely held belief that those who occupy the upper ranks of society have achieved that through merit, and others merely need to amend their ways; or, more accurately put, those at the top should reward those who reflect or mimic their pedigreed pathways. It's not dissimilar from telling youth of color that they need to develop grit to make it through the intertwined, systemic obstacles that intentionally impede their well-being and success.

While racism and patriarchy provide terminology and tools for naming these patterns of oppression, settler colonialism brings to light why these problematic structural patterns exist and the material investment expended to maintain them. Universities are able to preserve their image as the lever for social mobility through Band-Aids that ask more of populations who have already faced structural oppression, such as serving as "community representatives" on advisory committees. People of color are asked to convene diversity forums in which keynotes and workshops are provided, often where high-profile writers and cultural critics are signal-boosted as the marquee of the forum. While it is more than possible for a powerful talk, book, or workshop to set transformative learning into motion, this should not be equated with systemic structural and cultural shifts, nor with the power of collective mobilization. Even those spaces within the academy where land acknowledgments are read, statements that recognize a meeting or gathering is taking place on the unceded territory of specific Native nations, that does not put into motion the rematriation of land. Settler colonialism also allows us to see how the accumulation of debt and profit accrues in distinct yet connected stockpiles in higher education. Reckoning with settler colonialism obligates us to contextualize the claims from white students that they are somehow victims of discrimination because they are not able to participate in education initiatives for Black, Indigenous, Latinx, Asian, Arab, and queer students. Settler colonialism also reminds us of the ways that we've come to regard some knowledge as more valuable than the profound process of learning. Knowledge in a settler colony is touted through powerful speakers, leaving those who listen to the talk inspired and perhaps even destabilized. This, though, without a structural intervention, is a puff of steam that all too easily diminishes with time. Instead, the structure and creating alternatives, should take place in groups that study and act to create better shared living conditions for themselves and others. In fact, one of the salient lessons to be learned from study groups in social movements is that no high-paid speaker is required; only inquiry, texts, and people who study collectively.

THE PRICE OF ADMISSION FOR STUDENTS OF COLOR

Public institutions, including hospitals, schools, and government offices, are seen to be the goal and manifestation of a "developed" society. Ironically, the countries that are seen to be the least developed, particularly African nations, had the lowest rates of the highly contagious COVID-19 virus in 2020. The low rates could be attributed to public health infrastructures that simply do not exist in the United States, which led the world, sadly, in rates of infection and deaths from the virus. Although there are hospitals throughout the United States, easy and affordable access to equitable healthcare has been curdled by racial capitalism. In just this one example, developed societies are perhaps not so developed.

Education codifies the preparation of society's members through their ability to participate in that society's civic—meaning public—institutions. For example, you might have been placed in one of three or four reading groups in elementary school that was named a color or an animal, but you knew that you were in the low, middle, or super-achiever group. Tracking, as Dan Lortie described it decades ago, is determined by both formal assessments through testing and informal assessments that conflate appearance and obedience with intelligence.[21] In my public high school, civics was a required course for all seniors, and it was intended to be the last class where tracking was to be discarded, where students of all perceived abilities would learn as one democratic-like class about democracy. In US society, public institutions, particularly in the realms of education and the law, are said to be the backbone of democracy, in which the ability to engage democratically, through dialogue, is the manifestation of democracy itself. And yet, tellingly, my high school civics course only offered a vestige, a hollow gesture, to cross-cultural, including cross-class, dialogue, let alone collectivity. The tracks had been set long ago, and the young people in my class had long learned to seek shelter with who they had come to know through their parallel but separate experiences of schooling prior to this one class.

Although held up as symbols of advanced societies, public institutions are also creations of that society's values. As institutions, they institutionalize. Not to be confused with government or individuals who hold specific positions, institutions govern and create governance. Governance is the will, the impulse, and the preference of a nation-state. A student can attend a university and may well learn but not without being touched by the state's desired concept of a "good" student. The student enters into a debt relationship with the institution of higher education, and not just financially. The institution, by relegating the student to a number, one of many, also hones the student as a person in a queue, the object of rubrics and tyrannies of score averages. She may write papers for her courses but also becomes the writer of a series of emails pleading for overrides to enroll in a course, the release of work-study monies, a second chance when the first was squelched in schools that are still segregated and will remain so unless profound transformation is fomented. She is in debt. The university is her creditor.

This is starkly true for students of color, particularly those from working-class and working-poor families. First-generation students wrestle with imposter syndrome as they take classes and often work to pass as a member of a higher social class, if not to fit in with their peers then to at least avoid undesired attention. As with their professors of color, they are asked to serve on committees so that diversity is represented. The optics of diversity is the goal, and if they move beyond representation to vocalizing dissent or collectively articulating the need for structural change rather than reform, many universities are quick to reprimand them, call them uninformed about how much the university is doing to address racism—or more commonly, co-opt the issue and host a forum about it, after which little further action is taken.

It has become almost de rigueur after a racist incident occurs on campus for a university president or spokesperson to proclaim that racism has no place on their campus. However, both personal experience and myriad research shows that not only does racism have a place on virtually every historically white campus; it also exists on Hispanic-serving institutions, of which today there are more and more. As early as 2002, scholars such as higher education administrator Patrick L. Valdez and ethnic studies and education scholar Renée Moreno began questioning the ways in which the growing enrollment of Latinx and Chicanx students in higher education did not automatically mean that these students were being served by the institution, particularly when the faculty ranks and processes remained rooted in white patriarchal patterns of governance. For example, although the lowest-ranking schools within the University of California system enroll the highest numbers of first-generation Black and Latinx students, large class sizes and lower financial resources for students who are working while pursuing their degree perpetuate the trend of inequitable education. It is also often precisely these campuses where students vocalize their dissent after observing the dissonance between their lived reality and the promise of equity. I taught for a short time at the University of California, Riverside, and in the summer of 2020, when both the global pandemic of COVID-19 and legalized and extralegal murders of Black people sparked protests and anti-racist uprisings, one of those students sent me a message, saying, "You might not remember me but I was in your Winter 2018 class. We all still talk about that class and how we would not have the skills to understand anti-Blackness without having taken that class with you." While it is profound to receive such lovely feedback, years after a course has concluded, it also alarmed me that on a campus that is 86 percent students of color, there was just one course, at least in that degree program, in which they discussed anti-Black racism, what it means when we say that "until Black people are free, no one is free," and how beautifully dangerous Black and Indigenous sovereignty is to a nation structured through settler colonialism.

When students gather to protest, they are met with myriad responses. For example, in the mass of anti-racism protests that occurred in 2015–19, many student activists received varying responses from their institutions. The president of the University of San Francisco participated in a "die-in" on the campus, organized by students and faculty. The purpose of the protest action was to symbolically represent the four hours that the body of Black teenager Michael Brown laid on the street after being shot by Ferguson police officer Darren Wilson in 2014.

This demonstration, however, would prove to be an anomaly. In my research with student activists, many recounted less-than-allied responses from higher education administrators. Several spoke of being talked down to, being asked by administrators to provide a list of requests or to be "part of the solution" instead of only pointing out the problem of racism, or sexual assault, or transphobia. One doctoral student told me that she had been advised that participating in student protests would put her degree in danger, because she would not be giving it her sole attention. As a scholar dedicated to social transformation, I found this advice both off-putting and antithetical to the college's social justice mission, stated in every pamphlet and every page of the school's website. At best, this student was receiving mixed messages about what social justice meant. At worst, she was implicitly being told that social justice was merely a slogan and not meant to be a tool for interrogation and change.

In a discussion about his experiences in two different student-led campus uprisings in the late 2010s, a doctoral student succinctly explained the often irrational demands placed on students who call out inequities:

> It seemed to me a situation where students say: here's the structural issue [e.g., racism] but are then asked to provide advice, putting them in a position that is unpaid and relieving the administrator of their duties. As an example, a different structural issue, such as pipes leaking in a building, would, if following the same logic, be addressed by the administrators saying something akin like: "We had no idea about the leaks. OK, well, what do you think we should do about this?" You hire an architect, or a plumber, basically an expert. We've raised the issue. You're the administrator.[22]

This institutional response to student protest is cringeworthy both in terms of who it asks to do the hard and largely unprecedented work of dismantling racism, and how it shifts responsibility away from administrators. As has been documented in studies of higher education, some higher education administrators may have a scholarly background in management, but few are knowledgeable about the power relations created by and maintained through oppression, including the foundational and ongoing land and labor theft that colleges have carried out.[23] Neither are they familiar with the idea that when they are protecting their institution's symbolic value and bottom line, they are strengthening the tie between whiteness and property. Lastly, if they do know of the power of study groups and protests, their positions as representatives of the university typically dampen this knowledge, leading them to stay on message, representing the university's interests.

Higher education has also long been a slippery creditor of neighborhoods and communities. It began with land grant institutions. The credit extends into the current boom of defense contracts to universities. In 2018, 175 research grants and contracts were allocated

to institutions of higher education to support national defense infrastructure and software.[24] Additionally, there is an increasing
development of urban "eds and meds," the nickname for research-
intensive universities and their medical centers established in urban
areas. The debt and credit relationship of higher education to land,
neighborhoods, and communities has always been a complicated
one. Higher education has become one of the largest private sector
employers in many cities including Los Angeles, New York City,
Boston, and Pittsburgh, the city in which I did a great deal of the
study and oral history interviews for this book.

Pittsburgh, long known as Steel City, was a symbol and operating site of industrialization as well as unionization. Well before those
days, though, Pittsburgh was part of the Ohio Valley and Appala-
chia's network of resources for the Underground Railroad.[25] When
automation economies rose in the 1940s and lasted for decades, the
industries of steel and coal plummeted. Pittsburgh revamped itself
through the eds and meds formula beginning in the 1990s, then
moving on to coalesce alliances across university and healthcare sectors in the early 2000s. Now associated more strongly with its many
universities and medical centers, this city that is 26.5 percent Black
refurbished itself, and it did so by displacing many working-class
neighborhoods. In Pittsburgh, the traditionally Black neighborhoods
that experience the most challenges regarding public transportation
access as well as surging housing prices due to the encroachment of
employees of universities and medical centers have the highest rates
of un- and underemployment. Urban sites for universities and their
medical centers were the first deep-pocket entities to cross into government red-lined areas from which Black Americans were meant
to be restricted. Redlining, a once-formal legal policy that now con-
tinues in de facto practices, denies housing loans to Black peoples,
forcibly creating neighborhoods segregated by race. However, as
time progressed, the once-redlined neighborhoods became sought

after as sites for highly priced temporary housing, bought for condo owners and the purpose of renting the property for guests who might stay three to four days. Besides the loss of intergenerational neighborhoods, these changes in zoning and skyrocketing housing costs also meant the ongoing displacement of once solidly Black neighborhoods, with working-class Black and brown families pushed further out into the suburbs even as they still worked in the city.

A similar phenomenon has occurred in other college cities, as Davarian Baldwin has noted.[26] Caught up in a complex relationship with its community, residents of Harlem organized the 1968 "Gym Crow" protests. Columbia University had created plans for a racially segregated recreational facility. At the time, jobs were scarce in the then still predominantly Black west side of Harlem. The residents of the area cautiously supported the university's plan to expand seventeen acres of the neighborhood to establish a $6 billion research center. Before proposing the plan for expansion, the university collaborated with the city's planning departments and released a report about the "blighted" areas of West Harlem and Manhattanville. The report primed a justification for redevelopment of large portions of Manhattan. Columbia purchased $280 million worth of land, mortgages, and residential buildings in Harlem and Morningside Heights, setting the stage for the eviction of nearly ten thousand residents over the next decade, 85 percent of whom were Black or Puerto Rican.[27] Multiracial residents of Harlem and nationally known activists such as Stokely Carmichael showed up to protest the gymnasium, but more fundamentally, the swallowing of West Harlem that had displaced thousands of residents.

In a 2008 press release about the latest expansion, Columbia stated:

A thriving system of higher education is essential to preserving New York's historic role as a place that provides good middle-income jobs for a diversity of local citizens—and as a global center for attracting the great minds that make a difference in our society. What's more, through the public amenities included in this state plan and other commitments, Columbia's long-term growth will deliver a broad range of new civic benefits and University resources to those who live and work in our local community.[28]

Creditors create debt to profit from it.

In 2016, eight years after this statement was issued, when only a few initial steps had been taken for the expansion, the average rent for a one-bedroom apartment in West Harlem was $2,875 per month. In 1990, it was $650 per month. When I was writing one day in a café on 137th Street not too long ago, I was one of two nonwhite people in the crowded space next to a Harlem Children's Zone school, a charter school in what used to be P.S. 338. The Harlem Children's Zone is another multi-sited charter school venture that has come to play a profound role in education and property in New York City. Its name adorns many buildings in Harlem, and its wraparound services for Black families, while initially lauded, have come under valid criticism because many students and families are excluded from receiving them. Moreover, the practice of converting public schools into privately owned charter schools has become an investment opportunity for hedge fund managers who have no interest in education itself but are interested in the dividends generated by highly valued property in Manhattan.

The same block where I was writing in a café was a central location for the Harlem Renaissance in the 1920s. That cultural, artistic, and political movement yielded a bevy of publicly accessible art and social commentary by the likes of James Baldwin, Langston Hughes, Zora Neale Hurston, and Countee Cullen, to name just a few of its prominent Black artists and scholars. The nonprofit While We Are Still Here has knitted the oral histories of residents of two specific buildings in Harlem, on Edgecombe Avenue.[29] These buildings in the early and mid-twentieth century would come to house Black artists and cultural workers, including Drs. Mamie and Kenneth Clark, whose "doll" study remains a groundbreaking empirical study of children's early susceptibility to white supremacy. Harlem is a neighborhood made up of many little neighborhoods that have known brilliant Black joy and artistry, the ravages of poverty and drug wars, and, most recently, encroaching gentrification. Gentrification, a contemporary word for erasing to replace, unhouses not just people but also their histories. While no neighborhood or place stands still, neither should we be forgiven the debt of knowing what came before.

A DEBT RARELY SPOKEN

Although rarely acknowledged, the nation owes a great debt to the many cultures it has exploited for the purposes of accumulating property as whiteness. This is blatantly obvious in the ways that stolen labor built universities on stolen land. However, there are other forms of debt that are rarely framed as such. The nation owes debts not only to those who have suffered under its project of settler colonialism, but also to those populations who have manifested, under challenging obstacles, success and stability.

Nikole Hannah-Jones, a journalist focused on education and race, wrote a long-form article for the *New York Times* in 2015 that queried how the relatively small Xavier University of Louisiana had been able to train and prepare its Black students to apply to medical school and become physicians, far exceeding the numbers from any other college. The answer lies in the ways this historically Black college in New Orleans was guided by the principles of collaboration and refused to entertain the idea that there were not enough Black doctors because of an inherent lack of competency. Xavier's longtime president, Norman Francis, knew that the low numbers of Black students in pre-med tracks had nothing to do with their intelligence and everything to do with the substandard education that they had received in their elementary and secondary schools. So Xavier dispensed with a still widely used and overused tactic of weeding out students. Francis and key faculty at Xavier decided that no longer would teachers in a lecture full of first-year students use the tired cliché of telling students to look left and right to their classmates beside them and know that one of them would not make it through the first year. Instead of promoting competition and the process of weeding out those who did not immediately perform well on assessments, this HBCU decided to change its culture to one of collaboration and close attention to each student. It established early-alert systems so that well before the high-stakes midterm examination, students and faculty could move into action to support students who were encountering concepts that their counterparts in wealthier school districts had been learning in high school and from well-paid tutors. The school focused on large group study sessions and lifted up students who mastered the content quickly—not to exalt them, but to connect them with students who needed further assistance. To put it mildly, Xavier swam upstream in the waters of individualism, competition, and territoriality.

The debt that this nation owes to Xavier and many of the dozens of HBCUs in the country is certainly financial, as salaries at HBCUs are significantly lower than elite historically white schools, but the debt reaches beyond that. Without HBCUs, the nation would not be able to claim that upward social mobility has happened. In other words, this settler colony benefits by proxy from the buffer of community vision and cultural investment that HBCUs provide for its students. Currently, though, HBCUs remain underfunded and compensate their faculty at lower rates than elite public and private universities that are historically white institutions. This pattern was established by the second Morrill Act in the 1850s, and to date, there has not been political will to change these economic imbalances.

Despite having lower financial resources, the historical and on-going fight for civil rights, including equitable education, is also indebted to these schools, in many ways. It was the graduates of HBCUs, including Julian Bond, Thurgood Marshall, W. E. B. Du Bois, and Zora Neale Hurston, to name just a few, who called on this country to reckon with its practices of segregation for the preservation of white wealth and property. Education also owes a debt to the centering of learning processes, as evidenced by the instructional approaches in many HBCUs. More commonly known in education research as "culturally responsive pedagogy," HBCUs have long practiced teaching students about their histories, starting well before the holocaust of slavery.[30] In most Eurocentric curricula, the narrative starts with the arrival of Black peoples to the Americas. However, at HBCUs, through deep study of Africa and the African diaspora, students learn about their own histories. They do so without being surrounded by statues and paintings of slave-owning white men from the 1800s. Instead, they are steeped in the realities, including the vicissitudes, of their cultural heritage. A Black graduate student explained to me that when he commenced his doctoral studies at a predominantly white university, he was confused by theories such as critical race theory and racial capitalism that articulated the long-standing project of white supremacy. In his HBCU, there was no mention of these frameworks, as the central focus was Blackness, not whiteness as property.

Higher education has much to learn from HBCUs as well as other projects of self-determination. The Wôpanâak's language reclamation project is a grounding example of the rigorous study and commitment it takes to revitalize a language that had almost been vanquished. In 1993, Jessie Little Doe Baird had a dream in her ancestral language and it drove her to commence a language reclamation project. At the time of this writing, there is a school, created by Wôpanâak peoples, taught exclusively in their home language, and the curriculum is based in the foodways traditions of these people who were the first to encounter European settlers. Higher education may learn that its responsibility, its indebtedness, is to those who have always striven for learning and knowledge, rather than property and wealth.

CHAPTER FOUR

FUGITIVE LEARNING IN A SETTLER SOCIETY

I talk to my mother every day, but before I call, I always look at the clock. No matter the time zone I might be in, if it's noon in the plains of Turtle Island, I remember that my mother is watching the long-running soap opera *Days of Our Lives*. Like sands through the hourglass, I came to know my mother's intelligence slowly, cumulatively, in part because she had believed the malignant fictions that were furtively and overtly communicated to her for years. As a child, I listened to my mother belittle herself, not because she lacked a sense of worth, but because the world had consistently told her that a migrant woman who spoke English with an accent could not possibly be intelligent, let alone brilliant. It didn't matter that she taught herself English, a language with a completely different alphabetic code than her home language of Gujarati, slowly and over years. Neither did it matter that she taught herself to sew, and slowly grew a home business that began with hemming pants on a lone Singer sewing machine that she still has and uses, then expanded to owning multiple industrial-grade sewing machines to handle sizable jobs involving drapes, valances, and bedspreads. Nonetheless, it took some time before she was able to override the predominant narrative that she was not smart because she was a migrant, a woman, and spoke with an accent. The narrative that people with accents or who speak in vernaculars other than standardized American English are not as smart is insidiously pervasive. It shows up in soap operas like *Days of Our Lives* and well beyond. When Joe Biden commented that then presidential candidate Barack Obama "spoke well," this was a spin on the myth of African American Vernacular English being inferior, not actually a language unto itself. One of the migrant students I worked with in Boston put it this way: "Just because I speak with an accent doesn't mean I *think* with an accent." However, the pervading meritocracy narrative in the United States tells us that if we are good people, follow the rules, and work hard, that the American dream will open up for us. In this case, following the rules means being able to speak standardized American English fluently.

Narratives don't just tell a story; they structure material realities. Even though my mother managed to raise three healthy, personally fulfilled and professionally successful children in a home in which she was saddled with my father's addiction and emotional abuse, she never considered herself to be smart. Despite so many facts to the contrary, her story is testimony to the power of pervasive narratives that materially shape peoples' lives and life pathways. These narratives hold tremendous power even when they don't have a basis in reality but rather in the specter of domination.

Nigerian author Chinua Achebe wrote that there are malignant fictions and there are beneficent ones.[1] Malignant fictions are those that perpetuate falsehoods such as racial superiority; beneficent fictions are those that ignite a "self-encounter," in which readers face themselves and how the world sees them. Perhaps even more important than my mother's experiences with malignant fictions about her worth is what happened in her years as an elder that lowered the power of malignant fictions. No longer did she need to worry about taking the path of least resistance out of the hope that the vicissitudes of an erratic husband would quell more quickly for their children.

At the age of seventy-seven, she started to attend tai chi classes at a senior citizen center. This was truly the first activity that she engaged in whose sole purpose was to bolster her well-being. Before that, even when she had taken up the craft of sewing, it became a vocation that brought money into the house when we desperately needed it. She was and is a brilliant designer and craftsperson with fabric, but what became a desire to keep learning quickly became an essential livelihood to support the household. English, sewing, tai chi—all of these chapters in my mother's life are testimony to the ways that, despite coming from a village where girls did not attend school past sixth grade, she pursued learning all her life. Despite pervasive narratives about the role of women and the bigotry against migrants, my mother was able to puncture through these narratives, literally changing her material daily realities. She learned out of necessity and, more fundamentally, because learning is part of being human. Our integrated mind, body, and soul changes across time and contexts, so learning is integral to being alive.

The stories that we tell about ourselves, our people, our nation, other people, and success or failure all have material force in the shape and functions that institutions perform in society. Because higher education is a key place where settler colonialism is conveyed, it would be a profound mistake to overlook the learning that happens beyond and within education that departs from settler principles of individualism and property ownership. My mother learned to sew through apprenticeship. I have learned how to be in a loving political collective through my invitation to be part of that collective. We have to both decouple learning from schools, to be historically accurate to the many study groups gathering at this moment in homes and online, and to draw attention to the malignant fictions that are told about the nation itself.

In most US history books, the invasion of European settlers, often described as a "discovery," is coupled with renditions of how the United States began as a cluster of colonies established by a small group of people seeking religious freedom. Then, after a brief and amicable initial contact with the Wôpanâak peoples, Europeans, through treaties with Indigenous peoples, established the nation and expanded it well beyond the Atlantic seaboard. In fact, the journals of the first European invasion contain remarks reflecting admiration for the knowledge that the Wôpanâak peoples practiced. Through the lens of colonization, these observations were revised to essentially categorize all Native peoples as savage and without skills, a pretext upon which the settlers could claim the right to extinguish, or "civilize," them and their lands. Christopher Columbus wrote in his 1492 journal:

> They came to the ship in small canoes, made out of the trunk of a tree like a long boat, and all of one piece, and wonderfully worked, considering the country. They are large, some of them holding 40 to 45 men, others smaller, and some only large enough to hold one man. They are propelled with a paddle like a baker's shovel, and go at a marvelous rate. If the canoe capsizes they all promptly begin to swim, and to bail it out with calabashes that they take with them. They brought skeins of cotton thread, parrots, darts, and other small things, which it would be tedious to recount, and they give all in exchange for anything that may be given to them. I was attentive, and took trouble to ascertain if there was gold.[2]

This passage speaks from the vantage of what can be gained from this encounter. The last sentence is particularly telling. Although Columbus found no gold, what he and other settlers found was land, and over five hundred Native tribes living in relation with that land. The first encounter between the Wôpanâak peoples and Europeans quickly set the stage for the violent erasure of people, extraction from the land, and enclosure of peoples for profit. And that erasure has failed. Native peoples are here and will be in the future, despite settler colonialism's project to erase them to replace them with settlers who own property.

For many people reading the more common, malignant fictions about the start of this nation in K–12 instruction and seeing it perpetuate into what counts as objective knowledge in college, learning has often meant engaging in practices that are outside the gaze of whiteness, learning as a vital part of survival. In her 2020 book, *Linguistic Justice*, Black studies and linguistics scholar April Baker-Bell discusses the beauty and joy of Black English.[3] She notes that when two Black people who share a spoken code use that code in the presence of a white person, it is strategic. Baker-Bell's analysis is not just about contemporary interactions but about sociolinguistics practices that have been built, maintained, and utilized as strategies for survival. Not dissimilar from how education historian Vanessa Siddle Walker describes the trickster practices of Black education leader Horace Tate, practices that are both sophisticated and furtive, Baker-Bell provides context and contemporary research of Black youth enacting sharp analyses that are not found in their school curricula.

According to most US history books, Westward expansion, the era of European exploration and self-proclaimed ownership of land west of the original thirteen settler colonies, was accomplished through an imagined sense of duty and obligation to tame a "wild West" and establish trails and railroads that settlers could use to claim their parcel of "wild" land. The claim for land necessarily involved the removal of Native Americans who were "wild," in part, because they were intertwined with those lands. In the same history books, slavery is presented as a specific and unfortune moment in history, but then Abraham Lincoln came along, tussled and tossed about how best to save the nation, and to that end, ultimately decided to write into law de jure freedom for enslaved peoples. This put an end to the Civil War, thus closing that chapter of history, erroneously framed as a fight over states' rights. From there, the history books proceed through Reconstruction, the Industrial Age, the wave of European migrants in the late 1800s, two world wars, perhaps a bit of the 1960s popular culture,* and, depending on its print date, the election of the nation's first Black American as president. Throughout this narrative of the linear evolution of the United States, settler colonialism is rarely mentioned, and that absence works to perpetuate its power. In fact, it is possible, likely probable, that students who learn this narrative of initial European invasion might think that after the first few meetings on Cape Cod, the Wôpanâak peoples simply retreated from their homelands of millennia, as so many Native people would say: for time immemorial. To be sure, the word "invasion" is rarely used in middle and high school history books; instead, these settlers "landed" on Turtle Island, which they knew as "America," as renamed by Christopher Columbus, and all Indigenous peoples as "Indians."

However, viewing this narrative from a few steps back, several things become apparent about these events. First, these events are presented as a sequence, a development and divine evolution whose ongoing stated purpose is a just and equal society. Put simply, it is a linear story of meritocracy.

In that linear story of how the United States came to be a world power, there are a number of revisions and intertwined narratives that work to wallpaper over the violent realities of settler colonialism.

---

*It is telling to note that "popular culture" does not appear as a term in most US history books until the 1960s. However, popular culture existed before—one example is the postcards of lynchings that circulated in the late 1800s and early-to-mid 1900s. White supremacy long had its own popular culture texts and public spectacles.

First, manifest destiny, the God-given responsibility to tame savage lands and its peoples, itself carries the connotation of both an organic and divinely directed unfolding of a powerful nation. Second, linear progress is a predominant theme throughout. In most secondary school history textbooks, it is known as the era of "Manifest Destiny."[4] The linearity of these malignant fictions is, including what is omitted, a component of the urgent need for settler colonialism to provide stories that protect the reality of the structure.

However, at every stage of this smooth, linear story there have been fugitive practices by those being erased or contained. During the internment of Japanese Americans, "literacy was one of the ways that they [imprisoned Japanese Americans] resisted what was called iron fence disease, writing, creating and performing art," literature professor Gail Okawa writes.[5] When it was illegal for Black enslaved people to be literate, adults traced the letters of the alphabet in their children's palms. Linearity is a narrative, but the continuity of struggle is a reality.

Tapping elegantly into the narrative of linear progress, then First Lady Michelle Obama, addressing the Democratic National Convention in 2016, remarked, "Every morning I wake up in a house built by slaves. And I watch my daughters, two beautiful, intelligent young Black women, playing with their dogs on the White House lawn."[6] The reaction to this statement by an accomplished Black lawyer, raised in a middle-class family on the South Side of Chicago, vacillated between two extremes: joy at hearing the reference to the role enslaved peoples played in building so many of the nation's heralded buildings, and an almost equally loud and vociferous denial that the White House had been touched by the holocaust of enslavement. At their core, these reactions were at odds regarding not only the facts about the labor that built the White House but also about how much progress had been made in the time since it was originally built. Michelle Obama's comments were a clear reference to progress and advancement, conveying the spirit of the oft-referenced quotation by Dr. Martin Luther King Jr. that "the arc of moral universe is long, but it bends toward justice." In fact, President Barack Obama had the quotation woven into a rug in the Oval Office. However, Michelle Obama's gesture to progress must reckon with the fact that hours after Barack Obama was elected the nation's forty-fourth president and its first African American president, three white met set fire to a Black church in Springfield, Massachusetts. The church was burnt to the ground, land that was and is ancestral lands of Native peoples. Racial progress is intertwined with the resurgence of racism and the ongoing erasure of Indigeneity.

From mainstream textbooks, we don't learn that upon European settlers' first impressions of the Wôpanâak and other Native peoples were then rewritten to justify taming them through Christianity and European knowledge.[7] Not accidentally, this rewriting of original impressions served the purpose of narratively justifying settler colonial seizure of land. Settler colonialism quite simply would not work without the steady maintenance of narratives and celebrations, such as Thanksgiving, that reseat malignant fictions. However, these fictions are regularly unhoused, principally by the simple fact that the people who are depicted as temporary parts of the United States have survived generationally, despite attempts to erase them or collapse their humanity. Even those who perished through colonization remain alive through the beloved phrasing of young Black people who proclaim, "I am my ancestors' wildest dreams."

The perpetuation of the myth that race is a biological phenomenon categorically served the purposes of rendering Black, Indigenous, and other people of color as belonging to groups that are other, less than human.[8] Through codification and de facto practice, Black and migrant peoples were counted, in the former case, as chattel, and both were exploited as dispensable labor. Indigenous peoples, who were harder for settlers to classify into a single race, were deemed unilaterally savage and best served through enclosure, dislocation, and physical and cultural genocide.[9]

In specific moments and structures of society, this narrative of linear progress and hierarchies of humanness, because they are so widely held, retold, and re-instantiated, have had durable material effects. In various societal institutions, active forms of settler practices permeate lived consequences. Studies show that doctors routinely underestimate the amount of pain that Black patients are experiencing and that teachers often perceive their Black students to be older than they are, essentially erasing their childhood.[10] Erasing childhood, as Carla Shalaby points out, opens the doors wide for harsher punishments and overdiagnosis of socio-emotional maladjustment, and it robs children of the ability to play and be loud and inquisitive. This anti-Black racism is connected to the attempt to make African bodies fungible, no longer human, but simply property that should follow rules, without question.

When doctoral students are confused about what theories to use in their work, I often remind them that theory is a way of making sense of reality and that it has been part of telling reality through story for millennia. A young child's tendency to repetitively ask a single question—"why?"—asks for a theory in a one-word question. Theories tell us why things are the ways that are. Additionally, who gets to ask why and the generational answers, also known as knowledge systems, are systematically rewarded and erased through settler colonial education systems. The knowledge systems of those embedded in the highest strata are rewarded and the knowledge systems of marginalized peoples are erased in most of formal education. The high prevalence of erasing childhood and perceiving Black children as older tells us that while we may allow specific children to play and be loud and be inquisitive, we punish others for doing the same with disability labels, expulsion, and other forms of enclosure. But as long as colonialism has existed, so have efforts to oppose it, operate outside of it, and refuse it.

SETTLER COLONIALISM AND FUGITIVE LEARNING

Settler colonialism creates distinct yet connected relations of power for living beings, and it has, through the seizure of land and chattel slavery, served as a third pillar of the nation's institutions, alongside the church and the state.[11] Brown University's first Black president, Ruth Simmons, was also the first head of an Ivy League institution to institutionally and publicly convene a gathering in 2001, shortly after assuming her leadership role, to address the ways that Brown and other Ivy League colleges had been built through enslaved labor and have maintained extractive relationships through their employment practices. This action in and of itself was an intervention into Brown University's collusion with a slavery-based economy. Brown's sizeable endowment is undeniably tied to its profit through racial capitalism. It is located in Providence, Rhode Island, one of the primary ports along the Eastern seaboard where enslaved peoples who survived the middle passage were sold into a fresh new hell. Four hundred years later, echoes of racism as merely a thing of the past persist, signaling a desire to paint a picture of progress.

In 2019, *New York Times* education reporter Nikole Hannah-Jones designed and curated a special issue of the *New York Times Magazine*, entitled "The 1619 Project," which refers to the date of the first arrival of a ship carrying enslaved Africans on the shores of what would be later named the United States. In an interview on *The Daily Show*, South African late-night comedian Trevor Noah asked Hannah-Jones about the timeworn line that Black people should "get over" the history of slavery.[12] Hannah-Jones deftly replied that no one would like to get past the impact of slavery more than Black people, but its afterlife persists in the form of structural barriers to their wellness. Black studies scholar Christina Sharpe's renowned book, *In The Wake*, poetically delves into the depths of what it means for Black peoples to live in the wake of the holocaust of slavery, including the complex ways that descendants of enslaved peoples experience the full expanse of being alive while reckoning with an ongoing project that dehumanizes them.[13]

LEARNING AS FUGITIVE

I aver that we have much to learn about learning itself and that much of that organic education must come from beyond brick-and-mortar schools. Without a doubt, I became and remain a teacher because I was raised by a woman who never stopped learning. I ask you to consider how often learning has been undertaken in this settler society as an act of fugitivity, a figurative flight, a hidden practice, or set of small, furtive actions. The reason why is that access to learning has been withheld or denied, leading it to wither for many peoples. Furthermore, US law has explicitly criminalized long-standing practices of being literate and sovereign, or relied on cultural practices in schooling that stripped people of their languages and home knowledge systems.[14]

In the 2018 film *Black Panther*, one of the main characters is the nation of Wakanda.[15] Wakanda itself is an enactment of fugitivity. From the view of mainstream media, as depicted in the film through a twenty-four-hour news channel, Wakanda is yet another downtrodden, corrupt, and destitute African nation. Beneath this narrative and beneath the media's view of the nation, though, Wakanda is a technologically advanced society, one in which the elite military guard is all female, and Blackness is the norm. Killmonger, a Wakandan who was separated from his land and ancestors early in his life, temporarily claims the Wakandan throne through a ritual battle. He then loses this place of power and attempts to flee. Upon capture, still in the kingdom of Wakanda, Killmonger refuses the offer to stay from the kingdom's now-reseated king, the Black Panther.

Killmonger perceived the offer as tied to an existence in which he would not be free. He proclaimed that he would rather die like his ancestors, at the bottom of the ocean, than to be kept in chains. Killmonger is referring to the enslaved Black Africans who transcended language differences to stage mutinies or jumped overboard from slave ships. Their acts can indeed be considered a form of fugitivity, along with the many enslaved peoples whom Harriet Tubman literally stole back from slavery and guided to abolition territory. The US government had to grapple with fugitivity and enacted not one but two Fugitive Slave Acts—the first in 1793 and the other in 1850, which legally obligated people in the United States, including those in the free states, to return escaped enslaved peoples to their purported owners. Fugitives, in those government acts, were considered both property and, upon flight, criminal. One has to wonder how property, allegedly an entity without agency, can then become criminal, which requires the exertion of agency. This is but one example of what Cheryl Harris, as discussed in chapter 3, described as the shapeshifting and often tenuous distinctions that US law has made in the interest of whiteness as property. As these legal wrangles have been created, learning has also always been present.

Because learning was foreclosed to so many, fugitivity has necessarily had a strong connection to learning, throughout the history of this settler nation and other colonized places. When enslaved peoples were legally denied literacy, the teaching of the alphabet and literacy continued, secreted away through many means, including the poetic action of an adult tracing the letters of the alphabet onto the palm of a child. In her exhaustive and robustly researched book on the educational leadership of school principal and politician Horace Tate, Vanessa Siddle Walker presents a comprehensive history of the explicit and furtive tactics that Tate and other Black education leaders in the South used to create quality education for the region's Black children.[16] Walker describes Tate's work as taking both explicit and surreptitious forms, so as to keep from full view the strategies that put Black children into contact with well-resourced classrooms. Siddle Walker's portrait speaks of an educator whose commitment to quality education was part of a larger view of social transformation that had been pursued by generations before him. As just one example from this stunning text, Walker explains one of the lessons that Tate received from his mother. Tate recalled that he must repay the sacrifices his mother made under the heel of misogyny to educate Black children. In an interview conducted by an unknown interlocuter, Tate recanted a message that his mother told him to learn and keep:

> The new mother, as she looks at the head of the babe in her arms, whispers in her heart: "My child, may you seek the truth. And if anything I teach you be false, may you throw it away from you and go on to a richer truth and a greater knowledge than I have ever known. If you become a man of thought and learning, may you never fail with your right hand to tear down what your left hand has built up through years of thought and study if you see it not to be founded on that which is [true]. . . . Die poor, unknown, unloved, a failure perhaps. But close your eyes to nothing which seems to them to be the truth.[17]

In the space of this chapter, I cannot do justice to the deep ways that Tate heeded this advice through the heavy lifting of organizing, explicit partnerships, covert collaborations, and ongoing political education. He did this, of course, not as a sole individual, but as a driven leader who fought and strove for the education that Black children deserved but never received from schooling, a fact that persists to this day. Then, as now, the nation's institutions of formal education emaciate Black, Native, and children of color, often from low-income families, through underfunding and teachers who do not see them as fully human. Just as profoundly, Tate also had a high regard for knowledge and learning as intricately connected to life itself. In today's high-stakes assessments and nonstop testing, learning itself becomes subservient to achievement and ranking, thus abruptly blocking the ability to learn, live, fail, and try again. Learning becomes emptied of its worth and catalytic power.

Relatedly, Black, Indigenous, and people of color are told regularly about their worth, often without words. They are told through their surroundings, the substandard schools and the neighborhoods that have been depleted of resources. They learn about themselves as narrated through the Eurocentric curricula of schools and universities, and in the succession of funded research interventions that dabble with them and then leave when the funding ends. They are susceptible to learning that they are lesser or that they do not even exist. Inaccurate histories are presented as impermeable truths, and their power is strengthened with each reprinting. As a self-determined Black woman and experienced teacher said to me, in reference to the first and foundational course of her doctoral program, "There is one week. One week when we are supposed to read a few articles written recently by Black scholars. This course starts with John Dewey. That tells me that this course doesn't know who I am, doesn't want to know, and is satisfied with starting educational research with one white man and inserting its one week of *diversity*."

And yet, learning has, I argue, never yielded fully to this settler project of colonization of the mind. From the counterculture lessons taught within homes to social movements that used explicit direct action, political and self-determined education has regularly involved careful study as part of the project of changing the opportunities to literally learn and live for children of the darker nations. During the nationwide and global uprisings in 2020 in response to several killings of Black people by white police officers and white self-armed men, the city of Minneapolis was in the spotlight, as

Ferguson had been in 2015, along with so many other communities. However, long before this display of brutal anti-Black violence, MPD150, a community-based investigative and public scholarship group, was documenting the harm done by a militarized, largely white police force as well as the steps it has taken to disarm and take Black life.[18] Their work, which is not attributed to one single person, is freely available online, and has steadily served as a forum for public pedagogies about the struggle for life in the clutches of white supremacy. It is a fugitive praxis.

When I commenced to learn more and document the relationship between study and struggle, I had the great fortune of already knowing many activists, and was put into contact with many who are living legends. Karen Taylor, an artist, writer, activist, and good friend of mine, told me that I should talk with Ruby. Sure, sounds good. When I received an email from Ruby Sales, I gulped. Ms. Sales, a revered icon of the civil rights movement and an activist who uses spiritually grounded practices in her ongoing commitment to liberation. When we sat down on a chilly afternoon in 2017, she inquired about me and my project. I described it briefly, and she asked me if I had always wanted to be a researcher and writer. I responded yes to being a writer but only gradually accepted the researcher part, as I try to build knowledge that is mutually beneficial for all involved, including those yet to be born and those whose legacies we live within. She told me that it sounded like I had it figured it out, and we talked for two hours. About education, about white supremacy, about the long road of freedom struggles. When I asked Ms. Sales about how she came to be a political educator, she explained:

In systems like the Southern fascist education system, it's incorrect to assume that there's one system—without understanding that there's a counterculture, and the counterculture functions very differently than the dominating culture. And so, within this counterculture of education that I grew up in, we say that it was a long train running towards excellence. And right in the glare of the most brilliant fascist Southern apartheid, Black people engaged in the community project that began in 1863 immediately after emancipation, where Black men met in southern Alabama. There they placed the utmost endeavor to educate the youth for advancement of the race, for the preservation of rights and liberties. And those three aspects—no matter where you are, they universalize the projects that happen in countercultures. That there's a correlation between educating the youth which represents continuity, stability, and the future. That project was the engine of the Black counterculture of education.[19]

Sales's words correlate closely with the generational responsibility and dedication to learning in the face of overt oppression. Her experiences also speak to the ways that fugitive learning, or, in her words, counterculture education, is essential to the formation of ongoing struggles for life and liberties. Education scholar Jarvis Givens asserts that this learning represents "the enslaved person . . . (and political tension) at the heart of Black education, a project that dwells on the question of freedom and has historically required a fugitive disposition toward the dominant schooling norms."[20] Decades before, educator and historian Carter G. Woodson referred to this as learning as a means of escape.[21] For so many Black Americans, learning itself was an act of fleeing a schooling system and society that attempted to bar them from learning. Similarly, Native peoples have engaged in regenerating and engaging with the ways of knowing that had been steady targets of settler emaciation. In her book *As We Have Always Done*, Leanne Betasamosake Simpson explains that Indigenous resurgence is deeply integral in Indigenous ways of learning, being, organizing, and communing.[22] Throughout history, social movements have consistently involved education, particularly political education, although they have formed differently and been guided by different knowledge systems. Kelley's *Freedom Dreams* is a historical analysis of the ways that Black empowerment movements have done their political work, and the ways that the work often, if not always, involved political education.[23] In a 2016 essay, Kelley further explains, "Black studies was conceived not just outside the university but in *opposition* to a Eurocentric university culture with ties to corporate and military power. Having emerged from mass revolt, insurgent black studies scholars developed institutional models based in, but largely independent of, the academy."[24] Black studies, ethnic studies, and women's and gender studies departments were largely formed out of the campus protests in the mid-to-late 1960s. However, as Roderick Ferguson notes, these same programs, because of their visibility and dependency on the larger, corporate-like university structure, have ironically become co-opted into places of, at best, symbolic representation of diversity, and at worst, places where faculty and students receive the least amount of funding and support.[25]

This tendency brings us back to the advice that Horace Tate said he held closely throughout his life: be watchful of what is happening to what you have built, and be willing to destroy it if it no longer is serving the purpose of creating knowledge and educating oppressed peoples. Operating from a view that knowledge is static, narratives that create settler structures for the purpose of ownership are anchors for dominion, well-being, and wealth for a select few, coupled with risk, sickness, and accelerated death for many more, millions more. Although the nation boasts that it was built by immigrants, it also simultaneously conducts xenophobic raids and holds migrant children in cages at the border. What are we willing to destroy in order to restore, recreate, imagine into existence the ways we can be in right relation with learning, not for domination but for the sake of learning? I lay out this settler logic again here to underscore the dedication found in many iterations of fugitive learning as an enactment of life, as cognizant and tactically resistant to the colonizing bondage of body and spirit, and essential to projects of wellness for all living beings.

FUGITIVE LEARNING AND YOUNG PEOPLE

It is not a new finding that many, if not most, social movements have been initiated and emboldened by young people, people in their teens and early twenties. In 1968, fifteen thousand Chicanx students walked out of four Los Angeles high schools to create a rupture and demonstrate their objection to a curriculum that neither included nor addressed their histories or needs. The current social movement that we are in, closely tied to the Black Lives Matter movement, is no exception to that pattern. And as in the past, protests that started in the streets and in communities then percolated on college campuses. Just as with the University of California, as well as Kent State and Columbia University, to name a few schools and their respective regions where campus protests surged in the 1960s, they did so either after or in relation to the colonizing harms in the streets. Since 2015, campuses have been electrified with and by student protests covering a range of demands, including hiring more Black faculty, creating ethnic studies departments, and providing spaces for students of color to gather. Die-ins, marches, sit-ins at chancellors' offices, refusals to participate in athletic and academic activities—all these actions and more have been part of the groundswell of campus activism, the largest and most impactful since the 1960s. Youth and activism are not unfamiliar companions. Jay Gillen noted, "The great majority of fugitive slaves were young, roughly seventy-five percent between the ages of thirteen and twenty-nine."[26] Insurgent slaves would not tolerate political arrangements that left them enslaved, and eventually forced those arrangements to change. Similarly, young people today—whether recognized as political agents or not—defy educational arrangements that lock them into second-class citizenship.

Further, literacy learning as a fugitive practice often occurred in public spaces that the projects of colonization and indoctrination had simply not considered. One form of political and spiritual education that historian Rhea Estelle Lathan has written about is gospel literacy, which in multiple ways has been a long-standing and enduring articulation of Black cultural endurance and joy, both in relation to and differing from secular ways of knowing.[27]

In recent years, the Dreamers movement as well as the UndocuQueer movement have made information, research, and legal advice publicly available.[28] The Dreamers movement indicts the federal government's immigration policies that insist on deporting young people even though they are culturally American, with public protests in which young migrants proclaim that they are "undocumented and unafraid." Extending from that base, the UndocuQueer movement brings attention to the realities of queer undocumented migrants, lifting up the undeniable fact that intersecting vectors of oppression create different vulnerabilities. There is no doubt that a great deal of internal political education occurred before this outward public pedagogy could be used. Emi, a person who has for years been a core teacher in Summer Activist Trainings for young people, held in Southern California, offered her perspective on what it means to grow into activism. She started this work by connecting with Filipinx friends, listening to people's stories, and helping with outreach. In her retelling, she laughed, saying, "I didn't even know it was called outreach then." Emi has gone on to become one of the core Filipinx activists in Southern California, actively sharing and creating community spaces to learn about the history of colonization and how it has impacted the Philippine Islands, as well as the political resistance to this ongoing colonization.

For every march that happens, some political education and planning has taken place beforehand, and it has often included study and learning as part of those planning processes. For example, in the spring of 2015, I was teaching a graduate class called Critical Race Theory and Intersectionality, in which we read about and discussed settler colonialism. At its core, the course was a deep dive into the racist origins of the nation, along with the seizure of Indigenous land, life, and culture. As we met each week, reading about systemic racism and other forms of oppression that intersected to create distinct yet connected places of harm and vulnerability, Black people and allies were marching in Ferguson, Missouri. At that time Black Lives Matter became known across much of the country. As these students were learning about systemic racism and historical freedom struggles, it was all but inevitable that they would organize themselves and speak back to the entity that they had in common: their wealthy college. They studied racism and Indigenous erasure on that campus. They studied other student groups at different colleges. Some of them organized marches and die-ins, for which they were singled out and either disciplined or threatened with disciplinary action. That administration also asked me if I had required the students to organize as a course requirement. Of course, I had not, which was evident in the organization that included students whom I'd never met. More profoundly, though, that question was an insult to these students' grasp of institutional power, including their own.

In the aforementioned Kelley essay, he cautions us to avoid conflating youth at large with the young activists who are engaged in the political study that is so important for political struggle. In the course that I taught in spring 2015, there was perhaps a handful of doctoral students who decided to organize an anti-racist coalition. The other course members were in their own places of grappling with settler colonialism and racial capitalism as theoretical tools that required them to revisit the lies that they had come to love about this nation and, more specifically, their role in those structures. For some, activism might not ever be an option they would choose. In this sense, it is important not to conflate a social movement with an entire generation. In her biography of Ella Baker, Barbara Ransby makes a similar point: Baker did not work with young people simply because they were young. What guided coalition building was a shared set of politics.[29] In my own interviews with several civil rights leaders, they echoed the same point. Ruby Sales contrasted what she perceived to be a contemporary lack of rigorous study and debate compared to her organizing days in the 1960s:

> Well, of course a great deal of the movement was predicated on debating. We didn't just . . . for example, if we said that we wanted to have a march around the courthouse, the philosophical question would be what is the meaning of the courthouse? And does the courthouse have any more significant meaning than the black public school? And what is marching? Who really is in charge of that process? And marching—is it a hierarchy where somebody calls the shots and people follow? Is that a process where people . . . ? So, you go on and on for hours from a simple process like that with people really disagreeing and debating. And ultimately you come up with not a consensus but at least a comfortable space where you feel like you can do it, but it doesn't mean consensus because you never want to stifle the element of critique.

For Sam Anderson, a leader in SNCC, it was important to express that, more than a Northern or Southern divide, the internal political tensions and education was about the disruption of male dominance:

> In SNCC the role of sister leadership was keenly developed. Much to a lot of us brothers' reluctance, the sister leadership was key, was essential. You had the images of John Lewis and Kwame Ture, or Stokely Carmichael, wrapped around, being the public face, the

masculine public face of SNCC, but the day-to-day operations, the actualizing of the strategies and tactics—that was mainly the work of Black women, young Black women.

Anderson's comments about the leadership of Black women are fitting, because one of the important demarcations of Black Lives Matter is that it was started by three queer Black women. As Ransby notes in her 2018 book, *Making All Black Lives Matter*, because of the oppressions and wisdoms that these three women shared, the Black Lives Matter movement, from its start, did not have a place for patriarchy at its table.

Some of the activists I interviewed, who were most known for their work in the 1960s, expressed some cautions about contemporary social movements and what seemed to them to be a collection of actions that lacked a shared agenda created through debate and walking alongside people. And yet, we can see evidence of political research and tactics in the work of the Black Youth Project's We Charge Genocide and the Movement for Black Lives' policy platforms. The Dreamers movement's toolkits provide tools for creating local chapters of Dreamer gatherings as well as political education about the federal government's shifting immigration policies.[30] In fact, one of the challenges that older generations face in passing along knowledge in furtive ways is to do so with the understanding that historical, political, and cultural contexts change and will in turn change how fugitive political education and learning can and will happen.

FORMAL EDUCATION AND FUGITIVE LEARNING

In a time when privatization has been stealthily infusing every level of formal education with questions of efficiency over liberation, it may serve education researchers to consider how learning differs from achievement, particularly the form of personalized achievement that sets an individual's scores against their peers'. In fact, I propose that at this moment—with the encroachment upon and shuttering of public schools in Black and migrant neighborhoods; continued attacks on teachers' unions; the ongoing gaming of the school system, including that of admissions and test scores, by wealthy white people; and standardization of curricula—it is imperative for us to disambiguate achievement from learning.[31] In looking at social movements and the furtive, generational work to create quality education for children seen to be lesser from the colonialist perspective, it is vital that we learn from the work of study groups, and what learning requires and creates.

Learning is a potent, transformational praxis. Why else would a nation work so hard to delegitimize so many languages and even outlaw literacy for enslaved peoples? Literacy opens doors to learning and knowing. Those are fundamentally political practices because power is always present in who gets to know what. In fact, the university-based readers of this book need look no further than the current compromises to academic freedom to know that knowledge and knowledge production are always political. Tenure once meant having the academic freedom to pursue and write knowledge that may ruffle the feathers of those who hold more institutional power. It has become more of a salary guarantee and a revokable one at that. When I first earned tenure at an institution, I was told by an administrator that the university had in essence made a million-dollar commitment to me. I puzzled over that phrasing but not my immediate instinct to flee from it. After some time, I came to understand that as a public intellectual, I sought tenure not as a financial transaction but so that I could both continue to speak boldly and be in the room when other tenured professors debated whether to grant tenure to junior faculty, especially faculty of color. Throughout this process of coming to understand the explicit and implicit transactional nature of achievement in higher education, I also questioned what had happened to learning and the fact that all people are both teachers and learners.

When learning is engaged as a fugitive act, out of necessity, it should at once call our attention to disentangle learning from achievement and heed the lesson that learning happens well beyond a student's formal education—before, during, and after it. Traditional education desires students who will sit quietly for large stretches of time, be able to recant facts they've just been taught, and be in competition with each other. The long and varied traditions of fugitive learning shine a light on who is excluded from this formulation of education, while retreating from it to spaces where engaged discussion and dissent can happen. There is a tendency to romanticize the risks so many have taken over the centuries as tidy, linear stories of victory. Instead, the lessons from learning as an act of defiance, one that is undertaken not just for that moment but for learning to be possible in the future, is more circuitous and replete with covert and overt strategies. It is made by many and is not a single venture that can be credited to one celebrity.

Building on Tate's words about what we build and destroy, we cannot become so attached to what we are building for the purposes of equity and justice that we fail to notice that it is susceptible—at least to some degree—to simultaneously being corrupted and co-opted by long-standing vectors of oppression. In this sense, educational studies, while at risk in so many higher education institutions of a neoliberal winnowing of what counts as knowledge, have a tremendous role to play. Educational studies scholars and critical Indigenous scholars can and are bringing to historical study a critical genealogy of settler-state desires. These genealogies keep context and power relations central in repositioning learning as an active presence in all life forms. They are also raising up the authentic and purposeful learning that has been passed from generation to generation. In an article written and published during the COVID-19 pandemic, Ojibwe learning scientist Megan Bang emphasized the need for educators to re-consider categories, such as race, class, and gender, as well as theories that have become popular, for the purpose of asking what categories and new-ish theories can help us understand about when, how, and why learning takes shape. "I am working to cultivate a new rhetorical style in my own storywork that I hope will give rise to new pedagogical possibilities that emerge from generosity even for those who may not deserve it—for my own well-being and others'," she wrote.[32] Bang's intention and offering is staggering when I consider that so much of the harm that has been done to Native peoples is not known outside their circles, that there is an ongoing attempt to erase Indigeneity, and that she dares to utter these words to some who may not understand them. This is but one, albeit tremendous, example of the ways in which education scholars have engaged more and more with the dual realities of colonization and decolonization. It is within this field that questions of what counts as learning and for whom are essential questions. The fugitive practices of learning have much to teach us in the pursuit of those inquiries.

CHAPTER FIVE

THE STRUGGLE TO
STUDY IS VULNERABLE

"It is not enough to be right; you have to be smart."

—TA-NEHISI COATES, *Black Panther*, vol. I[1]

"Study is what you do with other people. It's talking and walking around with other people, working, dancing, suffering, some irreducible convergence of all three, held under the name of speculative practice. . . . The point of calling it 'study' is to mark that the incessant and irreversible intellectuality of these activities is already present."

—HARNEY and MOTEN, *The Undercommons*[2]

"We're hoping to meet with you at your convenience to learn more about your role within the School of Education and to talk with you about ways we might better reinforce to our faculty and staff the ways in which diversity, equity, and inclusiveness sparks innovation, builds resilient organizations, and leads to more informed, strategic decision making."

—UNIVERSITY OF PITTSBURGH ADMINISTRATOR,
personal communication, 2019

In my adulthood, I have had the fortune of learning from several powerful contexts: doing liberatory education work through teaching, continuing to be raised by movement organizing for education, and learning from the ways the universities still fall short

of knowing and speaking aloud their complex histories and current practices with settler colonialism. Working in formal school
contexts, both public high schools and universities, taught me a
great deal about the necessity and challenges of teaching for freedom and, as Bettina Love writes about, liberation.[3] As noted in the
decision to reopen schools in the midst of COVID-19's surging
numbers, higher education, with its foundation in settler colonialism, is now teetering into corporate culture, with companies like
Eduventures conducting market research for schools, and higher
education scrambling to find its place among fast-track and online
learning portals.[4] Working in these contexts, with talk of customer
service, along with the increasing need for faculty to find external
funding from nonprofit foundations and politically fickle federal
agencies, it is far too easy to lose sight and grounding in the relationships among life, learning, and liberation. It is therefore imperative to find side streets, under-passages, and pockets of possibility
for study.[5] Despite the multiple vectors of oppression that animate
themselves in schools across the nation, there is also the ubiquitous
presence of study.

Study, as this chapter's opening quote by scholars and artists
Harney and Moten describes, are dynamic spaces. One might not
consider that a conversation between two young people in between
classes is an intellectual exchange, but Harney and Moten guide the
reader to see that collective study about struggle is ubiquitous. That
conversation might be in Black English, which April Baker-Bell, and
before her, James Baldwin, remind us is not just a language but a language that is joyful because its mere existence is an act of defiance in
a society calculated on Black peoples' containment and demise. The
pockets for study are found in numerous places; but they are not
routinely reflected in the bureaucratic ongoings of higher education.
Harney and Moten are a thinking-and-writing duo whose work ap-
propriately transcends disciplinary boundaries. *The Undercommons*, a

publication that they have made freely available, addresses "under-commons" and side passages from oppression.

However, study is also vulnerable. Even not seeing it when we are involved in study makes it vulnerable. One of the first things Harney and Moten do is invite readers to understand the needs of higher education that stand counter to study as a form of struggle. In one example, they impress upon readers that the university desperately needs scholars who take a critical stance in their scholarship, scholars who write about power. This may seem out of keeping with higher education's intertwined history with settler colonialism and racist capitalism, but in terms of the institution's public relations needs, it fits perfectly. Even though faculty who do critical scholarship are regularly dissuaded from staying, the university needs to have the appearance of welcoming diverse theories of scholarship, so a revolving door is created for faculty of color.

It doesn't matter for how long, but universities need scholars to teach about theories such as ableism and settler colonialism. They also need those ideas that upend everyday narratives about the nation and its inequities to stay in the classroom. In this sense, what matters is enrollment, endowments, and public image. To be sure, there have been and are many higher education leaders who have carved channels for equity within the waters of bureaucracy.

However, transformative leaders are outnumbered by leaders who are more interested in the image of equity and their school's ranking rather than the complicated work of confronting inequities. The difference between these two forms of investment are brightly illuminated when the preferred public images of universities are infringed upon, such as through student protest that exposes how students often face discrimination based on race, gender, or ability. When these collisions of reputation and public protest occur, universities react: departments close and faculty are either fired, denied promotion, or strongly encouraged to leave.

In my own experience, when some students from my course on critical race theory in the spring of 2015 began to organize, I was asked to attend several meetings with the school's senior leadership as they sought to understand the source of the students' actions to squelch the protests. The administrators asked me if I had made the protests a class requirement. I repeatedly explained that I could not require anyone to become an activist, nor would I counsel these students out of their organizing. My years in community organizing with young people had taught me clearly that my role was to share what I knew of similar efforts and to get out of the way of their imaginations. But the die had been cast for the administration. In their view, by teaching a course whose curriculum was the study of the nation's origins and its ongoing projects of erasure and containment, I had created a problem. In Sara Ahmed's scholarship, she names this pattern more succinctly: if you name the problem, you become the problem.

When I was offered jobs at other universities with higher salaries and more support for my research, despite my established reputation as a respected scholar at that college and more widely, my college, in essence, shrugged at the offers. Universities routinely provide counteroffers to retain talented faculty, particularly faculty of color whose presence aids the university in its efforts to appear less racist. I was told that retention offers were not entertained, though I knew from several colleagues that this was an outright lie. Although I was a tenured faculty member, and the entire faculty of the Africa and African diaspora studies department signed a letter denouncing the failure to retain me, a nationally known critical education scholar, this paled in comparison to the threat posed to the white leadership, and perhaps most pointedly, the board of trustees and the wealth base of the university by the students' activism. Their organizing and actions were, in the minds of the administration, spurred by me and my own tussling with the administration, rather than their specific experiences and the reality of protests sweeping across the nation. To me, this only underscored the inability of a college with over $2.5 billion in its endowment to tolerate any power analyses that called it to task. Fortunately, I was raised by a mother who saw little value in status, and I was also politically raised as an adult by organizing for education justice. I left this college and have been fortunate to maintain employment as a public intellectual, but I share this snippet of tussling with university powers to underscore how the public teaching of the students' protests and the content of their demands were never a subject in the many meetings aimed at quelling their actions.

In organizing movements for education, I worked with community organizers, artists, youth leaders, and other school- and community-based educators, many of whom had never had a higher education degree but are the keepers of the stories of their people.[6] Through their method of teaching and being in relation through stories, they carry knowledge and make it available to the next generation. No tuition, no articles behind paywalls: just people, knowledge, and study. We met and worked to create spaces, defiant of the crushing, capitalist infringement on the fundamental right to education and the core human act of learning. Working alongside others in organizing for social change taught me about the advantages to be gained from justice-based premises for collectives and the durability of learning in study groups. We don't learn only the content; we learn how to speak as a contribution, not as a performance of our intelligence. It also taught me how liberation spaces can be creative, messy, synergistic, and complex.

Organizing also taught me, viscerally, that doing work for justice does not make any organization or collective immune from the many vectors of oppression, including heteropatriarchy, ableism, racism, and capitalist desire for attention. All of these vectors and more are both ubiquitous and baked into the power relations of a settler society. Unsurprisingly, even organizations and institutions that use the language of social justice also have oppression unfolding in those very same spaces. Centuries of carefully calculated strata defining who is not human do not collapse at the mention of the words "social justice" or "freedom." When harms take place, people often turn to restorative processes, including prioritizing the needs of the person or peoples harmed and building reparative conversations and actions over time. This itself takes a tremendous amount of time and labor. However, when undertaken by people skilled in responses to harm that do not involve punishment, people and organizations have the opportunity to learn how to create possibilities rather than resorting to containment and banishment. Restorative justice, in that context, maintains a systemic goal to address specific instances of harm, but from an abolitionist ethos that refuses carceral practices. In short, higher education and organizing spaces make mistakes, but they are very different kinds of mistakes and, perhaps even more tellingly, the responses to those mistakes are starkly different.

To reform, or more fundamentally revolutionize, the core purpose and intended audience of higher education, student pushback and protest has been crucial. For the most part, universities have only shifted their structural and cultural practices when students have demanded change to decenter whiteness and open opportunities for poor and subjugated communities. Too often, those changes are asked to be dealt with by people of color, often women, named as diversity workers. Implicitly, but also in plain sight through a system of referral to their offices, they are employed to absorb the racialized, gendered, sexed, and classed harms that students experience.[7] When students in the late 2010s demanded more DEI positions, this change made struggle for deep change vulnerable.

When students protested in the 1960s and the 1970s to demand spaces for minority students (to use the nomenclature of that era), to learn about themselves and their histories relative to these occupied lands, they used the tactics of sit-ins, protests, and public outcry echoing beyond university buildings. These protests led to the establishment of many interdisciplinary departments, including ethnic studies, Latino studies, Black studies, and women's and gender studies. In *The Reorder of Things*, a 2012 book by American studies scholar Roderick Ferguson, he traces the ways that these departments were created to take ownership over or co-opt the struggle for the university's own public image, as well as to contain the very potential for radically altering what counts as knowledge through mechanisms of the settler colonial structure of higher education.[8] As Harney and Moten write, the university needs scholars who employ theories that examine power in society, including scholars of ethnic studies, Black studies, and women's and gender studies, but it also emphatically needs those areas of scholarship to refrain from unhousing whiteness in the university.

Both moves, co-opting and containing, are linked through the shared strategy of acquiescing to just enough people and curricular programs so as to maintain a larger stronghold on white settler power, a move critical race theorist and law professor Derrick Bell in 1980 termed "interest convergence." Bell, in examining why the landmark case of *Brown v. Board of Education* came to be, asked this question: If the nation had been built on stolen labor and on stolen land, why would it suddenly have seen the light, so to speak, and changed course? He came to a different conclusion through examining a confluence of social phenomena after World War II, including the return of Black soldiers to a nation that still regarded them as inferior and the successful rebellion of many colonized nations in Africa and Asia. Bell posed that *Brown v. Board of Education*, which was meant to encourage racial desegregation of schools, was a gesture. A conciliatory act that would sacrifice a bit of power to maintain white supremacy as the cultural and economic stronghold of the country. Interest convergence, at its core, defines the convergence as widening opportunity just enough to stave off a more fundamental revolt, thereby maintaining the aggregate interest in whiteness as property.

Ferguson, through a steady examination of cultural moves in the mid-to-late twentieth century toward optically embracing minority difference, provides many examples of tenure denials and lower levels of material support for students and faculty of color. He also illuminates the ways that universities have often, after establishing departments for ethnic studies, women's and gender studies, and Indigenous studies, to name a few, quickly enrolled and contained these departments through the universities' own machinations. In other words, universities co-opt student protest demands and then domesticate and dampen the revolutionary potential of knowledges and cultures beyond the mainstream culture of individualism, competition, and achievement that relies on the façade of meritocracy.

The purpose of co-opting a demand from students is to prop up the institution as munificent. Students sometimes demand that a specific building's name be changed because of the history associated with that name. Universities can and have done this. The students who protested, for years, against the Silent Sam Confederate statue at the University of North Carolina at Chapel Hill were ultimately successful. However, despite students' knowledge of settler colonialism, UNC-Chapel Hill has yet to make any material moves to reckon with its settler occupation of Native ancestral lands. Containment is a way of fundamentally occupying the changes, such that they do not dismantle the order of power and the ordering of those who have power. From a settler colonial lens, this containment is in step with the pervasive and long-standing interest in containment as a form of power and domination. Naming social justice as an institutional ideal and disciplining counterculture spaces, as Ruby Sales deemed them, can, and have happened at the same time.

Upon its publication, Ferguson's book sent ripples through many departments created through the student struggles of the 1960s, bringing to the light the patterns of containment: interdisciplinary departments as the most frequent sites in which minoritized faculty were denied tenure, radical courses were buried through bureaucratic measures, and minoritized peoples suffered body, mind, and soul damage through the additional labor and political pressure that universities imposed upon them. As quoted in Ferguson's introduction, Adrian Piper, an anti-racist philosopher and conceptual artist, wrote to the then president of Wellesley College, stating, "I now realize that my inability to extend under these [hostile] circumstances of *professional standing* and *personal well-being* I had established before I arrived here is not due to my own failings, moral dereliction, or lack of motivation. It is the consequence of the paralyzing and punitive limitations Wellesley has repeatedly imposed . . . on the anti-racism work I have done both on and off campus."[9] Ultimately, Ferguson argues, these kinds of punitive efforts that universities directed at professors and departments hired and created, respectively, for their difference, have succeeded in keeping at bay "insurgent knowledges that would re-order material and social relations."[10]

Settler colonialism has been such a long-standing structure in the Westernized world that its ability to absorb, contain, and dilute demands for liberation and abolition should never be underestimated. The final quote at the start of this chapter is a message I received while acting as an associate dean for equity and justice. The language of "diversity and inclusion" has become ubiquitous across higher education. Since the protests of 2015 and 2016, openings for upper administrative positions such as the one I held for a time surged in numbers, ironically adding more to the top-heavy salary pyramid of higher education while other salaries stagnated, were converted into casual labor, or were furloughed. This further entrenched labor exploitation at the bottom of the pyramid: clinical faculty, adjunct faculty, and graduate students' labor. Another outcome of creating more upper-management roles is the containment of insurgency, as Ferguson describes, through neoliberal ideas of diversity for the sake of the "academy's transformation of minority cultures and differences into objects of institutional knowledge."[11] The purpose of such innovation, resiliency, and strategic decision-making is not named, but it is safe to assume that they, at minimum, prioritize the stability of the university itself. Diversity for the sake of innovation is a far cry from the core demand to dismantle obstacles to study. Struggle is vulnerable through the very ways in which its vocabulary is taken up and altered to serve the stability of institutions, rather than those most in need of stability.

THE PROBLEM WITH DIVERSITY

The centering of diversity is, in and of itself, a move on the part of whiteness, as it names the absence of "the other" as the problem, not whiteness.[12] Across college campuses, prior to and then intensifying after the protests of the 2010s, professional development workshops with titles such as "Difficult Conversations in the Classroom," "Dealing with Diversity Issues," and, to a much lesser degree, "Being More Inclusive" have been offered to a professoriate that remains overwhelmingly white. Despite these efforts, or more accurately because of them and their language failing to address white patriarchy, in 2017, Black women accounted for only 2.2 percent of full professors in the United States.[13]

Diversity has become a goal in and of itself; it doesn't seek to intervene, correct, and upend the harms of institutions of higher education built through and centered on whiteness as property. It has become a sort of pabulum goal for better learning and, more pointedly, a series of gestures that use a self-help-like approach to the entrenched, systemic issues of settler mentalities of entitlement, ownership, and dominion. Sara Ahmed's *On Being Included* delves into the reflections of diversity workers, those people who have titles or positions dealing with diversity.[14] The resounding themes are one, diversity positions are purposefully without the necessary power or resources to alter the racist patterns of the university, and two, these diversity workers are asked to be what I would term "cul-de-sacs." Their offices become places where students can go to air the discriminatory and often abusive experiences they've had, and the issue should then be resolved. At my school, I once told an administrator, who had asked me to attend such a meeting after I reported the harm that many Black male students were receiving from a tenured white female professor of statistics, that this approach of talking through the mythic "both sides of the story" is how couples counseling works. Systemic oppression, designed and maintained for settler colonial wealth, cannot be even approached through one-on-one conversations. Rather, these types of meetings perpetuate individualism and self-care sessions that are focused on the experience of being heard. These moves are important but incomplete. They should not be conflated with structural change.

After one of my doctoral advisees told me about the racism that he was experiencing in a required statistics course, I took action. I made sure that I had clarity about the statements that had been made to him, and how many times he had been called on for answers when this did not happen to other students, in essence surveilling his learning. I followed the chain of command and emailed the associate dean for graduate studies. That same afternoon, another associate dean saw me in the hallway and asked if I could meet the next day with him, two associate deans, and the professor who had made these comments. I replied that this was not a meeting that I needed to attend. I also knew, however, that if I did not attend and allowed my student's reputation to be sullied, absolutely nothing would be done about this form of regular, systemic racism. The way the meeting was set up was, in fact, a statement about the lack of understanding of systemic racism. I did not have a professional relationship with this professor; however, the meeting was presented to me as urgent and could not happen without my presence. The "couples therapy" approach to dealing with oppression is not how to reckon with centuries of entrenched realities of preferential admissions, which, contrary to the intended purpose of the legal ruling of affirmative action, has de facto worked to reproduce the same white, upper-middle-class culture within higher education.[15]

In fact, affirmative action itself provides an apt example of the ways that struggle is vulnerable. Its first contact with higher education was through President Kennedy's Committee on Equal Employment Opportunity. The committee raised the issue of the racial demographics of employees at the University of Michigan in 1962. The University of Michigan instituted an application procedure that did not ask for racial identity. In 1963, the university widened its policy of omitting race in employment applications to admissions.[16] From these initial actions, affirmative action became a strategy to account for the obstacles created for Black, Indigenous, and other people of color in applying to and attending institutions of higher education. Affirmative action has been a lightning rod in which the narrative of a "color-evasive" society, one that is shy to name racism in public proceedings, clashes with any attempt to contend with its racist settler foundations and present.[17] When affirmative action cases have appeared before the US Supreme Court, five separate times, each one opposing race-based admissions as an intervention into a system built for whiteness, the decisions ultimately upheld affirmative action, but each one has curtailed its focus and power from justice to diversity in service of better education environments.[18] Diversity itself has taken on a life of its own in higher education and in the corporate world, but what's remained consistent has been its use to evade confronting racism.[19]

VULNERABILITY IN PROGRESSIVE MOVEMENTS
The last decade has ushered in a large number of protest movements on the streets and on college campuses. Black Lives Matter, Trans

Lives Matter, #NoBansOnStolenLand, #TimesUp, and #Abolish ICE, to name a few local and global movements, have put themselves firmly in the public eye, calling for the cessation of harm to humans and other living beings, including the planet itself. These struggles are importantly different in their foci, approaches, and internal pedagogies. And yet, they are also mirrors of and windows into what education and American studies scholar Savannah Shange calls the progressive dystopia, the "perpetually colonial place that reveals both the possibilities and limits of the late liberal imaginary."[20] What does it mean to be a perpetually colonial place? What material, lived experiences come about from a late—meaning long-standing and perhaps on the brink of collapse—liberal imaginary? And isn't being liberal supposed to be better, more "woke" than being conservative or capitalist? Shange's phrasing brings up the difficulty that various movements for freedom from oppression experience. They struggle to see how they are distinct yet still linked under a settler colonial structure. When Shange refers to the late liberal imaginary, she is referring to this stage of racial capitalism, still in place but being called out and named through uprisings. An effective political imaginary, contrary to the liberal imaginary, ought to imagine a world altogether different, not one geared toward incremental change. Racist schooling, militarized racist policing, and a society that hates any threat to masculinity, so much so that Black trans women are murdered by other citizens with a disturbing regularity, cannot be nudged to be better through reforms. How can toxic masculinity be reformed? It cannot be. Its cultural momentum has to be shattered so that a society not so defined by gender and sexuality binaries can emerge.

This limit of the imaginary is one way in which the protests of the 1960s and 2010s share common ground in aiming for abolition of carceral logics of containment rather than incrementally nicer cages. There is no denying that the violence of militarized law enforcement on Black peoples has increased, along with the explosion of the for-profit prison industrial complex and the shuttering of mental health resources. Speaking to the linked logic of containment that runs throughout many manifestations of domination, activist and lawyer Talila Lewis rhetorically asked in an interview in 2019, "What do detention centers, prisons, cages, asylums, and circuses all have in common?" Lewis urges us to confront the deep and far-reaching obsession to containment and spectacle of those contained. Abolitionists such as Mariame Kaba, Erica Meiners, and Ruth Wilson Gilmore teach that a society predicated on containment is still based on relation, but it's a relation that numbs us to throwing people away, exploitation of the poor, population-level acceleration to death, and diseases incurred by polluted skies, water, and land. This undeniable reality forces us to face that we cannot ignore the planet's climate crisis, which has been forewarned by multitudes of Indigenous peoples, who understand land itself to be a living relative, rather than an inert resource to be owned and plundered for extraction. Confronting settler colonialism demands a reckoning that the seizure of Indigenous land to own it depends also on the use of enslaved peoples to cultivate that land. Racism relies on ableism and the rendering of peoples as less than human through the race "science" of eugenics. Enclosure and criminalizing migrants rely on defining them as wholly illegal, therefore illegitimate and unable to be protected by laws made for humans who have been anointed as such. These are inseparable projects. By struggling for migrants' rights without showing how patriarchy, land seizure, and anti-Blackness are intertwined, struggle becomes vulnerable to the kinds of empty gestures carried out in the name of diversity that only reseat settler colonialism by allowing it to hide behind one demand. These gestures are much easier to dole out when subjugated peoples are categorized into singular and separate groups. A common trend is to hold workshops divided into separate groups, usually racial and ethnic groups, with the assumption that people in that group have a shared set of experiences and definitions of justice.

We refer to "the Black community" or "the Latinx community," as if there are not widely varying experiences within these created categories. Education journalist Nikole Hannah-Jones pointed out in a tweet in 2019 that "the white community" is rarely named.[21] This is a case in point that these categories are creations, and more specifically creations for the purpose of whiteness. Whiteness does not need to be named, as it is both assumed to be the norm and when referenced it is more specific: ethnic whites, such as Polish, Irish, and German American people.* This pattern of sweeping pan-ethnic terms of the "Black community" or the "LGBTQ community" creates categories for the purposes of delivering differing but consistent messages of these groups' relationships to power and oppression. It also creates a challenge for people to work across the created categories for collective resistance and struggle. Consequently, settler colonialism trundles along.

RECKONING WITH STUDENT PROTESTS: THEN AND NOW

Universities often act or feign shock when a racist incident occurs and is proceeded by students' protests and demands, but history is always in the present. In an interview I conducted in 2018 about his experience of study and struggle formations in the 1960s, Ahmed (a pseudonym) spoke about his own growing awareness about universities and the creation of the Black Action Society, still in existence today at the University of Pittsburgh. The year, 1968, was in Ahmed's view the most racially volatile year in his life as an American young

---

*Notably, Irish migrants in the eighteenth century allied with Black struggles for freedom, as the Irish had been treated as expendable. However, they abandoned this alignment in favor of pursuing whiteness.

Black man in the United States. That was also only two years after the University of Pittsburgh changed from a private school to a public institution. As a newly public institution that had private monies, the university faced protests about its duty not just as a university but as a public one. Ahmed recalls that the formation of protests for a dedicated space in this public university, in a city regaled for its Black arts, for Black students on campus came about through informal political education.

One might assume that as students with access to the school library's significant holdings, they would gather there to find intellectual resources. On the contrary, Ahmed pointed to the political pamphlets acquired from bookstores in the traditionally Black neighborhoods of the Hill District and Homewood in Pittsburgh, geographically close but a great cultural distance from the college enclave in the Oakland neighborhood. These pamphlets articulated the pan-Africanist principles of Ghana's first president, Kwame Nkrumah, and cited Nikki Giovanni's poetry as the textual basis on which a number of students organized themselves, made demands to the university, and ultimately left their alma mater as changed human beings. However, Ahmed was also quick to point out in our conversation that his political education began at home, learning quickly that money and power "go hand-in-hand." This strikes a similar chord to the political education that Horace Tate received from his mother, with the advice that he must not hold tightly to ideas if they turn out to be insufficient. Tate also learned and modeled ways to gain political power while holding private political strategy sessions.

Similarly, Ruby Sales, the well-known civil rights leader and committed member of the Student Nonviolent Coordinating Committee, notes that she "grew up in a counterculture. In systems like the Southern Black culture, it's incorrect to assume that there's one system without understanding that there's a counterculture and that the counterculture functions very differently than the dominating culture. And so, within this counterculture of education that I grew up in, we say that it was a long train running towards excellence."[22]

Both of these civil rights activists, who still work toward the goals of equity, justice, and freedom for all oppressed peoples, had additional thoughts about the relationship between youth and education, more specifically emancipatory education. They, along with a founding member of the Black Panther Party I interviewed, expressed concern about the current Black Lives Matter movement's structures for communication and shared learning. The Black Lives Matter movement has often called itself leaderless in order to interrupt hierarchy and the elevation of individuals, often men, as the face and voice of collective social change movements. Related to that concern, Sales distinguished between hierarchy and authentic leadership. As she put it, "Your ability to lead was not conveyed upon you because you had a college degree. There had to be a correlation between your leadership and the project of liberating the people. This included creative artists, dedicated parents and committed students who would grow up to be committed, authentic leaders."[23]

The internal, informal fomenting of protests and movements regularly involved political education. It was part and parcel of the student public protests in the 1960s and 1970s. The debates of the Student Nonviolent Coordinating Committee, thoroughly documented in Ella Baker's personal papers, were a cornerstone to any action that would take place. From allowing photographers to document their work, to debating whether and how to accept donations from white benefactors, every potential move was widely debated among the members within chapters. Organizing also included fundraising to cover travel costs for regional and national meetings, which enabled members to share across localized efforts and knowledges. Only after rigorous debate and referring again and again to the purpose of the movement would action took place. However, as important as this priority for internal deliberation and how it happened was to SNCC, it is not this author's role to elevate one social movement's procedures over another one. Context is an active agent in how social movements are formed, who is involved, and what effects, temporary or foundational, they have had in the public imaginary of education, freedom, and liberation. It matters that many of the young adult protesters in the 2010s and through 2020 had been impacted by a sharp rise in mass shootings by white men, the scrolling images and videos on their smart phones of spectacularized Black death, and a nation that largely allowed such killings to occur with impunity for self-deputized and militarized police forces. This is not to say that the US activists in the 1960s or the protesters in 2020 in Nigeria had not themselves known that state violence is routinely exonerated. Instead, it is to point to the particularities of time and place that then show up in what is studied and what is demanded.

There remains that strong correlation between internal political education and external public action, or public pedagogy, today. The Dreamers movement, working for the humanization and rights of migrant youth, has dozens of chapters across the United States. In an interview about the relationship between civil rights and the narrative appeal of being "American except in one way," one of these youth leaders expressed the profound frustration of being caught in the web of what she knew to the thin narrative of meritocracy. "We know exactly how that messaging comes across, and we live with the decision, the strategy of fighting for each other, even though it means—and, you know, sometimes feels like—we are saying we are more worthy. But that is how this country thinks, not that we are here because of the danger in our home[lands] or what we went through in getting here, but are we good enough."[24]

Other youth and adult activists in both the Dreamers movement and Black Lives Matter movement discussed the ways in which conciliatory meetings with politicians and various policies sapped their energies. Ironically, much credit in the media of the Black Lives Matter movement is given to two men, both of whom have been at meetings held with presidential candidates and the White House, when it was three Black women—Patrisse Cullors, Alicia Garza, and Opal Tometi—who originated the phrase, specifically Garza, in 2014 on social media. Garza wrote a proclamation of love for Black people after unarmed eighteen-year-old Michael Brown was fatally shot six times by white police officer Darren Wilson; Patrisse Cullors added the hashtag #BlackLivesMatter; and Opal Tometi's work reminded all that anti-Black racism also impacts Black migrants. The public proclamation was a direct intervention into the foundational anti-Black racism of the nation, enacted through many vehicles, including militarized law enforcement. After Garza's post, protests sprang up across the country, with people proclaiming, "Hands up, don't shoot." Die-ins also occurred, with people laying down for four minutes, to highlight the four hours that Brown's body laid in the street before being removed. The protests after this and many other killings of Black people at the hands of a largely white police force have numbered in the hundreds since Michael Brown was shot and killed.

The question of leadership remains, for some, including many of the civil rights activists of the 1960s and '70s and the social movement agents of the 2010s. They are worried that the lack of visible leadership makes the movement more susceptible to patriarchy and government interference. However, this is not a unilaterally shared concern, but rather a manifestation of the very ways in which struggle knows itself and critiques itself.

VULNERABILITY IN DEMAND

Demand is active in many ways in social movements. The reason that a few Black men have been profiled more frequently than the three Black women who started the Black Lives Matter movement and its dozens of charters nationwide is due to the demand for a charismatic male leader. This echoes the largely unknown fact that Coretta Scott King was pivotal in politicizing her husband's views.

The demands of student protests in 2015, some of which Kelley critiques in his 2016 essay, asked for more Black faculty and students on campus but not necessarily shifts in power and funding. Notably, the 2020 strike by graduate students at the University of California, Santa Cruz, addressed economics head on. They demanded cost-of-living adjustments that had not been made by the UC system for years. The students waged their strike by refusing to fulfill their responsibilities as employees. UCSC fired the students, and ultimately rehired them. The UCSC protest is unique in its critique of racial capitalism as well as specific demands to redress exploitation. When I spoke to a student organizer who helped with similar protests at the University of Riverside, we both took a moment to digest that until 1960, tuition was free for California residents. Tuition at UCR now hovers close to $14,000 a year for undergraduates. This doctoral student poignantly said, "Damn, I'm in debt to this place that pays me less than minimum wage to teach. We need to demand much more."

The campus protests of the 2010s included such demands as the removal of statues of confederate officers and the portraits of former statesmen who were also enslavers. Students have also consistently demanded an increase in diversity training and diversity officers. Connecting to Sara Ahmed's scholarship on the "work" that diversity must do and is restricted from doing on campuses, these demands raise worries about conflating symbols with structural change. Symbols are undoubtedly important, acting as a form of narrative, and therefore affecting lived, often painful, material realities. At the same time, the removal of a statue is not enough. As just one example, the issue of who funds universities and what material interests those funds serve creates collisions in the pursuit of freedom for all. Only in late 2019 did Brown University declare that it would stop accepting donations from corporations that had violated Palestinian rights.[25] It has been historically true that to identify Palestine as a settler colony is to risk swift disciplining from academic institutions, such as in the widely covered case of the rescindment of a signed tenure contract for Professor Steven Salaita after he spoke publicly about the violations of human rights in Palestine.

The vulnerability in demand cuts many ways. In the case of Palestine, the vulnerability belongs firmly to the institutions who are fearful of these truths being spoken and the resulting financial implications. That perceived financial vulnerability led to Salaita's accepted job offer being rescinded. In other ways, struggles to study are vulnerable as they contend with centuries of individualism, patriarchy, and ableism. And vulnerability takes different shapes in different contextual times. In the student organization that was formed after some members took a class with me, that group confronted the commonplace patriarchy inherent in the pattern that women prepped materials, meals, and offered emotional support while men engaged in what was, seemingly, more intellectual work.

More than other demands, the media and some higher education institutions have hooked onto this generation's demand for safe spaces—literal physical spaces where they can gather and not be subject to oppression. Their demand stems from, as evidenced in chapter 1, the experience of racially minoritized students having what Harvard University had always called "house masters," and sitting in rooms whose walls contained portraits of university founders who were also enslavers. Routinely critiqued, and even mocked, as the cry from a "snowflake" generation, meaning they are too sensitive, safe spaces have become commonly dismissed.

In August 2018, University of Chicago dean of students John "Jay" Ellison sent a letter to incoming students, telling them:

> You will find that we expect members of our community to be engaged in rigorous debate, discussion and even disagreement. At times this may challenge you and even cause discomfort. Our commitment to academic freedom means that we do not support so-called "trigger warnings," we do not cancel invited speakers because their topics might prove controversial, and we do not condone the creation of intellectual "safe spaces" where individuals can retreat from ideas and perspectives at odds with their own.[26]

Ellison's statement on behalf of the esteemed University of Chicago both vastly underestimates the myriad experiences that take a personal and population-level toll on the well-being of minoritized students, and misconstrues the core purpose of academic freedom. For example, many minoritized students take humanities classes where their histories are told from the point of European encounter, or more aptly put, invasion and conquest. In the physical sciences, they may attend biology classes that sloppily correlate race, widely understood to be a social construct, with poor health outcomes, rather than explaining that those outcomes for Black, Indigenous, and People of Color directly result from racism.[27] Ellison's statement also ironically silences the ways that universities have long been places of harm and opportunism, under an ill-informed notion of academic freedom, for the benefit of an elite institution's still largely white male professoriate and student body. Ironically, the people who are being protected in this announcement are professors who ask their students to interact with research and theories that objectify subjugated peoples. Academic freedom has been collapsed into a facile notion of "free speech" and an articulation of "both sides of the story," when higher education itself has always been harmful physically, psychically, and spiritually to those cast on the underside of humanity.

As a woman of color who knows the history and ongoing hierarchies of power in the academy, I have never expected the university to be a safe space for me. But neither do I expect my students of color, particularly those who are at the intersection of multiple vectors of oppression, to simply endure curricula and practices born of white supremacy for the sake of so-called intellectual rigor. The standards for intellectual, emotional, and societal rigor require much more of universities, specifically from the people who are the best paid. The challenge should actually be reversed: to demand rigor from a power base miseducated through Eurocentric schooling, in understanding the knowledge systems in Native, Black, and migrant communities. For example, those in leadership need to do the critical genealogical work of studying how and why the phrase "nothing about us, without us" came from disability rights collectives.

In our internal political education conversations, I have always engaged students about the experiences of people like Adrian Piper, a public intellectual and artist who through word and image alerted her audience about the seductive disciplining that universities employ for brilliant scholar/artists whose work is fundamentally anti-racist, doing exactly what they were hired to do. She was routinely disciplined for her work. Piper situated these experiences as the harmful and unsurprising outcropping of a white settler institution that seeks to maintain the semblance of anti-racism but functions in racist ways, particularly toward women of color.

When they are overloaded with requests to be on committees and provide unpaid labor, I remind graduate female students of color, particularly Black women, that they are already succeeding in a society that uses both patriarchy and white supremacy to dismiss their deep knowledge. I remind my colleagues that "being a good citizen," a phrase often used to uphold demands for labor, should not mean sacrificing one's well-being from chronic stress. The hallowed halls are not safe spaces for BIPOC populations; they were never intended to be such. But that does not mean that we are not always studying in the spirit of Harney and Moten. Nor should we ever stop demanding better from these institutions, demanding them to be answerable to their histories and ongoing practices of exploitation for the profit of a few.

I, in fact, do want safe spaces, but in the sense that students and faculty can show up to a learning community with their entire selves. As Talila Lewis explained in the planning process for the 2017 Free Minds, Free People conference, showing up as one's full self means that when a person expresses a need to any institution, it should be received by that institution as an invitation to try its best to meet that need, not as an annoyance or an expression of disproportionate need. In fact, Lewis and other scholars such as Nirmala Erevelles have argued that ableism itself is a core expression of coloniality, seeking to create a dis/abled other in order to normalize a fictive stable set of human abilities.[28]

Perhaps the greatest risk in the struggle to study is that people will overlook the long-standing tradition of study groups for social change. Enslaved peoples long engaged in furtive acts to perpetuate learning. Black children in abolition schools in the free states protested the instruction they were receiving. As Ruby Sales reminds us, the people who began to dream into existence what we now know as HBCUs were those who, only days before, were considered chattel property under law. A fundamentally inhospitable institution has no chance of being a place of learning and providing full access to BIPOC of all genders and abilities even though it has "included" some of them. The last fifty years have reinforced that the institution, left to that theory of change, will shapeshift its positions and departments to contain, control, and dampen the upending that comes through liberatory learning.

CHAPTER SIX

STUDY GROUPS AND COLLECTIVE STRUGGLE

Theories of Transformation

"We're already here, moving. We've been around. We're more than politics, more than settled, more than democratic. We surround democracy's false image in order to unsettle it."

—HARNEY and MOTEN, *The Undercommons*[1]

"The honor, I assure you, was Harvard's."

—W. E. B. DU BOIS, upon being congratulated for being the first African American to earn three graduate degrees, including a PhD, from Harvard in 1895[2]

I read and reread the quotations above repeatedly. They *click* sometimes. Sometimes I'm perplexed at what it means to surround the false image (of democracy) precisely to unsettle. And then I remember the Chicanx high school walkout of 1968. Those young people, many of whom—if not most—were making their way in poor living conditions in families where underemployment and labor exploitation were the norm. The high school students organized internally to make a public demonstration that sought not just to disrupt the status quo to gain access to their own histories and cultures, but to educate. I have worked with undocumented youth in more recent

times, and their level of political analysis would challenge many
studying Marx's theories of capitalism in university courses to keep
pace with the lived praxis of challenging a settler system of relationships to maintain a power base for wealthy white populations. Truth
be told, I doubt many researchers are aware that when they tell the
story of an overachieving migrant youth, they are collapsing structural obstacles of racism and global capitalism, and strengthening
nationalist narratives of meritocracy.

The existence of a high-achieving young person should not be
cited as evidence that society-wide oppression has been erased, just
as the existence of harm at the population level does not mean that
some individuals won't beat the oppression odds. An Oprah Win-
frey doesn't erase the legal and extralegal killings of Trayvon Martin,
Tamir Rice, Laquan Johnson, Atatiana Jefferson, Pamela Turner,
and Sandra Bland, to name just a minute fraction of Black peoples
killed at the hands of police or self-deputized people. The fact that
the United States named the first Native American to be poet laure-
ate in 2019 does not erase the ongoing disappearance of multitudes
of Indigenous women.[3] The mainstream acceptance of Laverne
Cox does not erase the fact that in 2019, as of October 31, nineteen
transgender or gender-nonconforming peoples had been murdered.
By late 2020, the annual number of gender-nonconforming people
murdered had more than doubled to thirty-four.[4] Black transgender women are all too often abused and killed. They are targeted
for not only daring to cross and disregard the strict norms of accepted gender lines, but also because as Black women, they pose a
threat to masculinity's dominance, simply through their existence.
Racism cannot explain the simultaneous disappearance of Indigenous women, the epidemic murders of Black transgender women,
and the cultural genocide of migrants from the Global South. Confronting settler colonialism and its logics and actions illuminate how

disappearing Indigeneity is coupled with the gendered spectacle of Black containment and death.

CONFRONTING SETTLER LIES
When we say their names, when we articulate the histories and contemporary moves of colonization that have been the backbone of this settler nation, we may ruffle feathers. If that outcome is a primary concern, then we're already adrift of any project of transformation. The core purpose of naming the root of violence is to abolish it so that a better society may grow. When we say their names, and work together to think about the complex relationships with land that settler colonialism has created for many populations, we position those very populations, and their relation to each other and the land, as central to the act of agitation. We acknowledge the ways we are indebted to each other, not in terms of money, but in terms of interconnectedness. We act with the maturity it takes to understand the importance of telling the truths of those whose lives and histories have been squandered. We pick up the mantle for the struggle to study that has existed since oppression first created its metrics to deny access to learning to millions, as a way to deny their humanity.

This book, purposefully, harkens to the palimpsests through history that mark and echo both colonization and concurrent struggles for freedom. I have looked, countless times, at the picture of the Black Power fists raised by athletes Tommie Smith and John Carlos at the 1968 Olympics in Mexico City during their medal ceremony. In the iconic photo, they are shown heads bowed, with one fist in the air. That fist is synonymous with Black Power. Less noted, though, is that they also wore shoes but not socks, to convey the pervasive injustice of poverty and its intersections with racism. If there is a pre-eminent grand stage of patriotism and nationalism, the Olympics are surely it. As relevant then as it is today, Smith and Carlos's

silent protest and demonstration of Black Power exposes the mis-
match between the nation's claims to protecting human rights and
its work of oppression, both historical and contemporary. Lesser
known are the debates about this action that happened beforehand
and the attempts to dissuade the two men, as told by John Carlos,
from holding up the iconic Black Power fist. Carlos was advised by
a close confidant that the only time that fist has power is when it is
holding money.[5] As a people who have been dreaming and pursuing
freedom for centuries, Black Americans, like migrants, learn quickly
that ownership of a home, of property, or a business is the imprint
of the American Dream. They also, however, learn quickly that that
dream is less available to them because of the still elusive generational wealth that whites continue to hold in the United States.
The desire for stability through money is understandable, but as any
factually based history of whiteness as property teaches, the laws and
practices of anti-Blackness will do their best to unseat the economic
gains of racially minoritized groups to preserve wealth for a few.

Carlos and Smith came from shared and different backgrounds.
One had grown up in Harlem long before it became gentrified, and
the other was the son of a migrant. They had to decide quickly how
to show their dissent at the Olympics, but the move to action had
been in the making for months, if not years. Carlos and Smith had
been in conversation with their families, each other, and in study
groups. They knew that the 1968 Olympics would provide a grand
stage, but of course, they could not predict that they would both be
standing on the medal podium.

This history is crucial, as without it, it is far too simple to dismiss
this as a one-off, spontaneous action of dissent. Similarly, were we
to rely on the facile fictions of Rosa Parks simply being tired and
wanting to sit down on her bus, we would never learn about her
long-standing work as an organizer for labor and women's rights.[6]

Most US history textbooks, when they do mention civil rights activists, paint them as peace-seeking citizens acting in isolation. Rosa Parks was not a moderate or an accommodationist, but rather a radical feminist who had studied at the Highlander Folk School. History textbooks call her the mother of the civil right movement, but this quite simply is false. The Montgomery bus boycott, which is misattributed to Parks's single defiant act of sitting in the front of the bus, was preceded by months of study by many collectives. This study was connected to what people learned from centers like the Highlander Folk School, where education rights activist Septima Poinsette Clark taught after her contract was not renewed because of her activism in support of Black teachers and principals in South Carolina.

For all the references to Martin Luther King in textbooks and politicians' speeches, rarely is it stated that the famous 1963 March on Washington was for jobs, not racial unity. Singling out tidied-up histories of individuals facilitates the erasure of entire, multipronged study and struggle efforts, erasing the names, groups, work, and legacies of civil rights champions such as Bayard Rustin, Diane Nash, and Claudette Colvin. Study and struggle are historically linked to, and specific struggles are the result of, rigorous thinking and planning, just as the nation's power structure and its relations among settlers, Native, Black, and migrant peoples were intentionally built and purposefully maintained. Struggles for social transformation and their accompanying study are often found beyond the walls of formal higher education.

Some notable exceptions to study that reckons with the reality of settler colonialism do exist. Ruth Simmons, the first African American president of an Ivy League institution, publicly acknowledged the foundation of enslaved Black labor that literally built the campus, and created a forum for the study of this history.[7] To this day, new students at Brown University can take a tour of the campus that focuses on the harms committed by the institution. Referencing Simmons's initial gathering at Brown University, the Radcliffe Institute at Harvard hosted a similar gathering featuring keynote speaker Ta-Nehisi Coates among many other renowned historians. Coates, a National Book Award winner and later recipient of the MacArthur "genius" Fellowship, spoke to the ways that universities have engaged in ongoing plunder of Black people and communities. These events, in and of themselves, are not transformative. They are interruptions to Eurocentric curricula, but perhaps more importantly, they leave an imprint, however temporarily, that higher education must contend with its role in settler colonialism.

Freeman Hrabowski and his leadership in higher education took a different tactic than that taken by the large, high-profile gatherings. He chose to reverse the culture of individualism to one of collective success. This leadership is another example of a person in a position of power in higher education whose work for equity was concerned less about reputation and more about collective wellness. Hrabowski, a former Freedom Rider who learned from the practices of SNCC, shifted the purpose and culture of a higher education institution, and later in his life served as the president of the University of Maryland, Baltimore County. In that leadership role, informed by the collective resistance centered on the struggle to study in the 1960s, Hrabowski prioritized Black student achievement in math and science through collaboration rather than competition.

CONFRONTING SETTLER SYMBOLS

Symbols are a powerful force because they provide us with a tidy narrative of fairness and justice. I think of how professional football player Colin Kaepernick first knelt during the playing of the national anthem before a preseason game in 2016 as a silent and profound statement about the long-standing divide between the word of the nation and its ongoing violence on Black peoples.[8] The explosion of vitriol against Kaepernick's practice of kneeling should tell us something about the attachment we have to specific fictions and their politics. Fans' investment in white supremacy must have been profound if they rejected a player who had achieved so much for his team. Kaepernick's contract was severed. Some four years after his contract was severed, Kaepernick clarified, again, "I am not going to stand up to show pride in a flag for a country that oppresses Black people and people of color. To me, this is bigger than football and it would be selfish on my part to look the other way. There are bodies in the street and people getting paid leave and getting away with murder."

This talented athlete and student of Black history and culture made it clear that he was kneeling not to disrespect the nation but to symbolically make apparent that under one of the nation's most powerful arms, law enforcement, Black people and people of color were being killed. One of the most frequent, and relatively docile, critiques of Kaepernick's silent protest is that he was being unpatriotic and that the national anthem was "not the right time" to kneel as a political statement. I wonder if, in fact, we have a widely shared comprehension of what the word "political" means. For US citizens whose souls are stirred by the sound of the national anthem and the images of military personnel in formal attire, are they also similarly moved by China's anthem? My provocation here is that simply because a statement, song, or action is familiar to us, that familiarity does not make it apolitical. On the contrary, it has been made to be memorized and known so that the political narrative of this nation is refreshed each time it is sung in stunning fashion and accompanied by thousands in stadiums and watching at home.

In fact, throughout our daily lives, political symbols and actions surround us and are made more obvious if we can recognize them as purposefully politicized. Consider the slightly less subtle but perhaps even more dangerous erasures of Indigeneity that occur all around us. How many visitors to New York City stroll along Broadway without knowing that the pathway was originally marked and used by the Lenape peoples to tend, be in relation with, and steward that part of Turtle Island, long before European settlers arrived and drew imaginary borders to mark the settler nations of Canada and the United States? As I sit in my office at the University of Pittsburgh, a school with strong school pride, I wonder how many of our students, staff, and faculty know that one of the university's main thoroughfares, Bouquet Street, is named for Colonel Henry Bouquet, who oversaw the distribution of blankets infected with smallpox to Indigenous peoples in the 1760s.[9] This act was without a doubt an act of chemical warfare. Just one block north of the University of Pittsburgh's Oakland campus, Neville and Craig streets were named in honor of the wealthiest owners of enslaved people in western Pennsylvania at the turn of the 1800s. To name these realities and the ongoing erasure of stolen labor and stolen land should cause ruptures in the feelings of school pride, municipal identity, and patriotism that many feel. Again, poet Nikki Giovanni's words are grounding: that if we wait for a "good" time to tell the truth, we will never do it. It is always the right time.

Decolonial scholar la paperson, in his book *A Third University Is Possible*, brings forward the theorizing of Ngũgĩ wa Thiong'o, who proposes that the decolonial already resides within the colonial; that these contradictions abound and are part of the wind and force of ongoing colonization.[10] La paperson cautions against a tendency to overdetermine colonization in all moments and actions. The examined relationship between study and struggle speaks to the need to not overdetermine colonial education's hold on study. Neither should we romanticize and overdetermine the impact—or more pessimistically, the futility—of struggle. Struggle, flight, fugitivity, and even within-school success can be and have been acts of decolonial resistance.

REFUSAL OPENS SPACE FOR THE OTHERWISE

When Du Bois stated that his three degrees from Harvard were Harvard's honor, it was a deft act of decolonial refusal, succinct and cutting close to the bone, as the work of the best writers tends to do. Chicanx students, Dalit women, Indigenous water protectors, Black athletes who refuse to ignore the sins of a nation that profits from exploitive power relationships: all of these are instances in which we are invited to, as writer, artist, and scholar Ashon Crawley invokes, see and be in "the otherwise."[11] Otherwise moments, whether they are acts of refusal or the dancing that occurred during the 2015 protests in Ferguson, Missouri, are full of agency, brimming and spilling over with self-determination and joy. In other words, life itself. These actions defy the settler colonial desire to absorb peoples into projects of erasure and containment. Harney and Moten remind readers that within study is talking, walking, dancing, and shouting. In their poetic frames of study, they remind us that study is inherently part of being alive. Crawley draws our attention to how much otherwise is all around, stronger and more durable than oppression.

Moments of otherwise surround us constantly, but can we hear them, see them, feel them? The grinding machinery and power relations of settler colonialism often keep us so busy that we can barely hear our own thoughts, but the otherwise is always there, has been there, and will be there. Perhaps the hardest task we have in this particular time of study and struggle is to not conflate symbolism with the more transformative dismantling of power structures. While it very much matters that more deans of schools of education are Black in 2020 than ever before, this itself does not shift the material structures of racism that pulse through university processes of admissions, tenure, and grading. As a concrete example, having a Black dean does not mean that white male faculty will stop receiving the highest course evaluations. However, refusing to uphold these forms of evaluations would be a transformative action, altering security for those whom society rewards simply because they are white and male.

SYMBOLISM IS NOT TRANSFORMATION

As discussed earlier in this book, one of the key differences between the student protests of the 1960s and those of the 2010s is in the demands that students made. In the 1960s, students' demands were for dedicated spaces and curriculum for and about marginalized identity groups. They demanded material resources such as funding for scholarships, alterations to curricula centered on whiteness, access to each other's phone numbers, to name a few examples. The student protests of the 2010s, bolstered by the Black Lives Matter and #MeToo movements that, again, started beyond college campuses, have focused on material demands, but often in the form of diversity officers, removal of artifacts celebrating founding fathers who actively participated in the plunder of Black and Indigenous peoples, and the hiring of more people of color. This is, of course, not a comprehensive list of demands. It's still notable that the demands raised during the social movements of the 2010s have been focused more often on symbols and the desire for safe spaces. These are important, obvious demands, but the very nature of the time spent hemming and hawing over these changes should teach us something about asking for too little.

However, some notable examples show a path of both self-determination and a theory of change that creates more equitable practices while it indicts harm. In 2018 and in 2019, UCLA hosted gatherings called "Liberation Lawyering." Sponsored by more than a dozen campus groups and the National Lawyers Guild, the gatherings brought together activist lawyers and experts from many communities to delve into how the law, typically used as a mechanism of settler colonialism, can be used for justice. Attorneys who participated in "Liberation Lawyering" received credit for professional development, required to maintain their active bar status. Formal education requirements can be shifted for liberatory purposes. All the time.

Transformation requires a deep reckoning with power that perpetuates settler colonialism. The staggering example of the University of Missouri's football team's refusal to play another game of the 2015 season until the then president spoke directly about racist incidents on campus is such a reckoning. Within a week of their refusal to play another game, the president and the chancellor of the University of Missouri resigned from their positions. There is no arguing that that is material change, but systemic racism, one of the engines of settler colonialism, requires constant, nimble confrontations that work for and toward decolonization, abolition, and freedom. Put another way, settler colonialism has benefited from people conceiving of it as a historical event, not an ongoing structure and reality. That has allowed this overarching structure of society to stay under the radar of better-known perspectives such as critical race theory. In fact, when I started a critical race theory course at Boston College in 2013, I did so with the full intent of addressing settler colonialism. However, settler colonialism was less known as a theory or area of study than critical race theory. The first scholarly pieces about critical race theory in education were published in the late 1990s. Settler colonialism, in 2013, had not made its way into the field of education studies. Similarly, fugitive practices of study and struggle have been and must be nimble themselves, sometimes engaging in trickster actions of distraction to create space for study groups focused on the root of the problem.[12]

Higher education institutions will often cite the numbers of people of color who are students or faculty as a demonstration of inclusion. Boston College and the University of California, Riverside were featured in a 2019 article in the journal *Inside Higher Ed* for the uptick in faculty of color hired by each institution.[13] Although both claimed a large uptick, neither institution's spokesperson gave a specific number of hires. Instead, each attributed its success in hiring racially minoritized faculty to vague "best practices" such as the widening of search networks. What was not discussed was how many faculty of color were not retained beyond the lowest ranks and salaries, how many hours of additional labor these faculty put in working with students of color who seek and need guidance, and sometimes literal protection, from hazing and discrimination by race, gender, and sexual orientation. The diversity trope is subject to a tendency toward optics of representation in the form of, for example, reaching a specific quota, indicating implicitly but clearly that a certain threshold has been met. The desire for diversity has led to the creation of diversity workers in higher education. These diversity workers are also socialized into a frame of constantly being in debt to the university, as they often do not have the same political power as provosts, or even full professors, 78 percent of whom are white men. When they ask for money and material change, they do so at the whim of some administrators who have fallen for the hustle that putting a person into a diversity role provides an antidote to racialized, sexed, gendered, classed, and dis/abled harm on campuses. Typically, when a well-known scholar accepts a diversity and equity position, their signed contract is featured in the university's press releases on social media and in higher education news outlets. In a sense, those diversity workers are already working for the institution before they've been paid.

Articles that celebrate increasing diversity, as the aforementioned one about Boston College and the University of California, Riverside, almost always fail to address how many of these faculty are hired to teach courses that feature worn-out titles about multiculturalism, approach social justice as a widely held single goal, or focus on diversity issues in the classroom. Teaching these classes often encloses faculty and their curricula within the confines of what higher education scholar Dafina-Lazarus Stewart has called the "language of appeasement" diversity and inclusion, particularly as it applies to those who are lower in the ranks of institutional power. Diversity seeks optics and confuses those optics with historical knowledge, political acumen, and cultural transformation. Inclusion, to me, is just as dangerous and too small of a goal to reckon with settler colonialism. It does not address the fact that for decolonization to happen, people cannot be simply included into a settler project that is counting on the majority of them being killed or contained. These are perhaps the precise ongoing colonial moves that Ferguson warned about in *The Reorder of Things*. They also contain within and alongside them the possibility and probability for decolonization to happen, as la paperson wrote. Without contextually rich knowledge, which can only be undertaken by those living in specific places and gathering in specific spaces, the exact contours are, perhaps rightfully so, only deeply known by those in the moment. As Harney and Moten remind us, study is everywhere.

MOVING BEYOND SYMBOLISM REQUIRES STUDY

During the 1960s youth uprisings, there were many factions and approaches. In this book, I have foregrounded the work of Ella Baker and her peers, particularly Ruby Sales of the Student Nonviolent Coordinating Committee (SNCC). Their work was anchored in and beholden to a premise that to catalyze change for the better, we must be with the people who are, literally, risking physical harm to simply cast a vote. The research aspect of SNCC is woefully unheralded and under-chronicled. Not dissimilar from W. E. B. Du Bois's work in the late 1890s that led to the publication of *The Philadelphia Negro*, SNCC used multiple forms of research (surveys, interviews, geographic images), and time living alongside people to better know and listen to what they had to say about their lives.[14] This approach to organizing, as Ella Baker so often noted in infrequent public addresses, built up people's confidence to be their own leaders, to trust their own knowledge systems, and to work from and for generational strength.

Zora Neale Hurston, a writer, freedom dreamer, and anthropologist, took a similar approach with her research and her fiction. However, she received scorn for writing in the vernacular of Black Southerners of the mid-Atlantic. Hurston deigned to speak truth, as it was and is, casting aside the disciplinary trappings of a more acceptable, "respectable" form of dialogue, which would erase the cultures of Southern Black peoples. Zora Neale Hurston died in 1960, in cruel living and health conditions. Although she had learned from one of the premiere anthropologists of that time, Franz Boas, Hurston received minimal praise for her nonfiction and fiction works during her lifetime. Hurston's life story is similar to that of the prolific feminist Chicanx theorist Gloria Anzaldúa. Anzaldúa's work, particularly her book *Borderlands*, is at a canonical level. But what do professors who assign her work or the students who read the classic book learn of her struggles in life, particularly living with illness that was not treated due to the capitalistic nature of healthcare, just as it is today? Despite and arguably because she so clearly understood these material challenges, Anzaldúa wrote elegantly about one of the most pervasive and least discussed pillars of coloniality: identity categories:

I am often asked, "What's your primary identity? Is it Chicana, Mexicana, Mexican American, Latina, or Hispanic? Is it being a woman, queer, working class, an elder, short; is it being a writer, diabetic, intellectual, spiritual activist, mystic, dreamer . . . ?" This question assumes that a person can be fragmented into pieces like Coyolxauhqui, and I answer, "All of me is my primary identity. I can't be cut up like a pie, with each wedge assigned a category of identity." Like the genetic code, all of me is in each cell, and every single little piece has all of me. I am all of the above, but also more.[15]

TRANSFORMATION MEANS LOOKING WITHIN AND TOGETHER

In 2012, Eve Tuck and K. Wayne Yang published an open-access article entitled "Decolonization Is Not a Metaphor."[16] The article is exhaustive in citing and indicting the facile moves that are made in the name of decolonization, but which never address the issues of land, theft of labor, erasure of Indigeneity or arrivants, and the bamboozling of a subset of migrants into desiring unattainable whiteness at the expense of intersectional resistance. To put it mildly, Tuck and Yang's article shook the foundation of many who had proclaimed decolonization as a goal but had not thought about their relationship to occupied land or, more precisely, the rematriation of land, waterways, and the skies.

Tuck had in 2009 published an earlier piece in the *Harvard Educational Review* entitled "Suspending Damage: A Letter to Communities."[17] In this letter, written to Indigenous communities but with the full knowledge that it would be read widely, having appeared in a high-ranking journal, Tuck calls for a suspension—not a permanent embargo—of Indigenous communities viewing themselves through a damage-based lens. Attend almost any educational conference, and unless it is based in principles and practices of community and liberation, you will likely hear about various categories of peoples (Black, Indigenous, Immigrants, Queer, Dis/Abled) and the damages they sustain through an oppressive reality, specifically a settler colonial reality. Tuck does not ask readers to deny that damages have been done, but does ask that this not be the sole lens through which communities see themselves. She pushes readers to think about the implications of someone only knowing herself and her people as damaged and how that affects her humanity and her capacity for knowing what form of change is right.

Taking into account these historical and current struggles and articulations, I hold that struggle must involve study, that to study without struggle is to perpetuate the conflation between learning and school-based achievement through measures of whiteness. Society cannot change without struggle, and that struggle is susceptible to the kindling of appeasement that might burn but provides no heat or light.

There is no study without struggle. There is no struggle without study. Just as the palimpsests of freedom struggles in the past only benefited from study, so will those struggles to come. Study will make strides, it will endure attempts to be contained, and sometimes, it will be subject to the colonial moves of co-opting. One of the challenges is holding many spaces and places at the same time. Containment, bodily and psychically, operates at a population level. Both liberatory practices of study and struggle are planned through relationships and with intersectional analyses that allow intersectional resistance to multiple forms of oppression. Study to struggle is a population-level phenomenon, but it is always specific, growing through local, organic impulses to holistically learn about and then reassemble what settler colonialism has cast asunder.

Study and struggle for liberation requires that we unknow many falsehoods that are foundational to settler colonialism: categories of human and nonhuman,[18] land as inert, health as a luxury for a few, the pillaging of the planet and its darker peoples as the "natural" order of things.

Decolonization and liberation, when we pursue them, will push us to the of edges of how we have imagined not only justice but freedom. This is the same outcome Achebe believed was possible through the invaluable work of "beneficent fictions"; we'll encounter, as he predicted, edges we didn't know existed. Those are the moments when we must be grounded in the duality of study and struggle. Robin D. G. Kelley, one of the most rigorous historians of freedom movements, asserts that categories, created for oppression and in which we've made homes, must not be more important than freedom itself. He cautions us against overdetermining where we seek to create relation, interconnectedness, and actions to benefit many peoples, or what shape or form liberation and mutual solidarity may take. Kelley, along with la paperson, cautions us against overdetermining colonization. To me, this is the quintessence of the duality of study and struggle: releasing what one already knows in order to learn. That act of releasing is at the core of learning, letting go of what we are sure of, to reach for unknown possible futures beyond those of settler-driven ranking and separation. Kelley states:

> Solidarity is becoming increasingly distant in a political atmosphere that can only see white people as "allies" and not comrades, or only see anti-Black racism as the only thing worth fighting for, or questions whether or not Black people should support struggles of people who have not succeeded in quashing all vestiges of anti-Black racism. . . . Comradeship is not built on some metaphysics of race or some shared experience of oppression. Comrades are made in struggle, and they are never numerous and they don't necessarily look like us. . . . People of Color is not an identity but a relationship defined by racism, dispossession and imperialism. I'm not saying we're just "people" or making some claim to universalism, but rather we need to recognize that as long as "difference" is structured in dominance, we are not free and we are not "made." Making revolution requires making new identities.[19]

As a lifelong student and educator, I have long had an ambiguous relationship with formal education. I often tell my students that they should not seek love from the institutions that hire them or charge them tuition. Institutions don't define us, our relationships do. In light of my critiques of formal education institutions, including higher education, I am sometimes asked why I work within them. The answer for me is a simple one: I love learning. I love that it is hard, it is destabilizing, and, in its most transformative ways, it demands us to literally be different. Less individualistic, competitive, and punitive with ourselves and each other. Most fundamentally, I refuse to concede the catalytic power of study and learning to settler colonialism.

ACKNOWLEDGMENTS

As with all our work, it is never any single person's work. Since 2015, Rachael Marks has been a dream editor at Beacon Press, fighting for this book when "settler colonialism" was not a widely known term. Her sharp intellect and regular nudges of "more, explain, example please" helped this writer make the points clear and alive. In fact, Rachael was often able to probe in a way that helped me to see more precisely the point that needed to be made. I am also indebted to the team at Beacon Press who stay steady in their commitment to be a press for social change. Managing editors like Susan Lumenello make that happen in detailed reads. Brian Baughan is a person I've never met, yet his editorial work peeked into my thinking and helped me to say it more clearly. Wayne Rhodes, for years, read early drafts that resembled ramblings and did what he has done for hundreds of first-year composition college students in Boston: found the nuggets and encouraged them to keep writing, always keep writing. Thank you to so many students who asked to read drafts of this book and supported it with their labor, including Patriccia Ordoñez-Kim and Jawanza Kalonji Rand. Jawanza, in particular, worked with final drafts of this manuscript to help shape it into a solidly referenced resource so that it can be part of wider discussions about property, life, and learning. I am indebted to the generosity of the Murri, Lenape, Hawai'ian, Quechua, Cheyenne, Unangâx̂, and Wôpanâak peoples for being in relation with me.

I am grateful for the support of the Spencer Foundation, which allowed me to pay young and elder social movement activists monies for their time in telling me their stories. Although stipends are not unique in oral history projects, they were particularly important for this book, as so many of the activists who made time to speak with me did so out of love and as an additional form of labor and ethic resting on the premise that archiving knowledge is essential to social transformation efforts. However, often that labor is uncompensated. This kind of generosity is a mirror of the many ways that people have benefited from social movements without ever being a part of them. Spencer president Dr. Na'ilah Suad Nasir provided encouragement for this book when it was an idea. And, of course, without my circle of brilliant cultural workers who push my thinking, hold me in my struggle, this book would not exist. I am so fortunate to think, study, act, laugh, and live alongside my Education for Liberation family.

Finally, I cannot present any significant work without acknowledging my mother, truly one of the purest learners to have lived. She is the most autodidactic person I know. I recently told her that, and if I hadn't rushed to tell her what an autodidact is, I'm sure she would have, true to form, taught herself the definition. She knows that life and learning are inseparable. As with anything that I accomplish, it is because of her. When people ask me where I'm from, I say that I come from the fortune of sitting by my mother for decades and that I am half the woman she is.

NOTES

AUTHOR'S NOTE

1. Lindsay Peterson, "'Kill the Indian, Save the Man,' Americanization Through Education: Richard Henry Pratt's Legacy," honors thesis, Colby College, 2013.

2. Sandy Grande, *Red Pedagogy: Native American Social and Political Thought* (Lanham, MD: Rowman & Littlefield, 2004).

3. Stefano Harney and Fred Moten, "The Undercommons: Fugitive Planning and Black Study," Research Collection of Lee Kong Chian School of Business, Singapore Management University (2013): 1.

CHAPTER ONE: STUDY AND STRUGGLE

1. Becca Andrews and Madison Pauly, "Campus Protests Are Spreading Like Wildfire," *Mother Jones*, November 19, 2015, https://www.motherjones.com/politics/2015/11/missouri-student-protests-racism.

2. Brandon Griggs, "Do U.S. Colleges Have a Race Problem?," CNN.com, November 10, 2015, https://www.cnn.com/2015/11/10/us/racism-college-campuses-protests-missouri/index.html.

3. James Baldwin, "A Talk to Teachers," *Child Development and Learning* (1963).

4. Robin D. G. Kelley, "Black Study, Black Struggle," *Boston Review*, March 7, 2016, http://bostonreview.net/forum/robin-d-g-kelley-black-study-black-struggle.

5. James Queally, "Watts Riots: Traffic Stop as the Spark That Ignited Days of Destruction," *Los Angeles Times*, July 29, 2015, https://www.latimes.com/local/lanow/la-me-ln-watts-riots-explainer-20150715-htmlstory.html.

6. bell hooks, *Feminist Theory: From Margin to Center* (London: Pluto Press, 2000).

7. Rachel Herzing, *Political Education in a Time of Rebellion*, Center for Political Education, n.d., https://politicaleducation.org/political-education-in-a-time-of-rebellion.

8. "Transcript of Obama-Sotomayor Announcement," CNN, May 26, 2005, https://www.cnn.com/2009/POLITICS/05/26/obama.sotomayor.transcript/index.html.

9. Sonia Sotomayor, *My Beloved World* (New York: Random House, 2013), 38.

10. John F. Kennedy, *A Nation of Immigrants* (1958; New York: Harper Collins, 2018), 9

11. Kennedy, *A Nation of Immigrants*, 9.

12. Kennedy, *A Nation of Immigrants*, 9.

13. Darnell L. Moore, *No Ashes in the Fire: Coming of Age Black and Free in America* (New York: Nation Books, 2018).

14. Troy McMullen, "For Black Millennials, Student Debt Is the Biggest Hurdle in Homeownership," *Washington Post*, October 31, 2019, https://www.washingtonpost.com/realestate/for-many-black-millennials-student-debt-is-biggest-hurdle-in-homeownership/2019/10/30/6c06a300-e6a4-11e9-b403-f738899982d2_story.html.

15. Urban Institute, "A Five-Point Framework," https://www.urban.org/policy-centers/housing-finance-policy-center/projects/reducing-racial-homeownership-gap/five-point-framework.

16. Anthony Fry and Anthony Collufo, "A Rising Share of Undergraduates Are from Poor Families, Especially at Less Selective Colleges," Pew Hispanic Center, March 22, 2019, https://www.pewsocialtrends.org/2019/05/22/a-rising-share-of-undergraduates-are-from-poor-families-especially-at-less-selective-colleges.

17. McMullen, "For Black Millennials, Student Debt Is the Biggest Hurdle."

18. Office of Fair Housing and Equal Opportunity, "Housing Discrimination under the Fair Housing Act," www.hud.gov; McMullen, "For Many Black Millennials, Student Debt Is the Biggest Hurdle."

19. Brandon A. Jackson and John R. Reynolds, "The Price of Opportunity: Race, Student Loan Debt, and College Achievement," *Sociological Inquiry* 83, no. 3 (2013): 335.

20. U.S. Bureau of Labor Statistics, "Labor Force Statistics from the Current Population Survey," October 5, 2020.

21. Monica Coleman, *Making a Way Out of No Way: A Womanist Theology* (Minneapolis: Fortress Press, 2008).

22. Carla O'Connor, "Black Women Beating the Odds from One Generation to the Next: How the Changing Dynamics of Constraint and Opportunity Affect the Process of Educational Resilience," *American Educational Research Journal* 39, no. 4 (2002): 855–903.

23. Anthony P. Carnevale, Nicole Smith, and Jeff Strohl, *Help Wanted: Projections of Job and Education Requirements through 2018* (Lumina Foundation, 2010).

24. Joy James, *Transcending the Talented Tenth: Black Leaders and American Intellectuals* (New York: Routledge, 2014); Dafina-Lazarus Stewart, "Language of Appeasement," *Inside Higher Ed* 30 (2017); Robin D. G. Kelley, *Freedom Dreams: The Black Radical Imagination* (Boston: Beacon Press, 2002).

25. Craig Steven Wilder, *Ebony and Ivy: Race, Slavery, and the Troubled History of America's Universities* (New York: Bloomsbury, 2014).

26. Lani Guinier, *The Tyranny of the Meritocracy: Democratizing Higher Education in America* (Boston: Beacon Press, 2015).

27. Paulo Freire, *Pedagogy of the Oppressed*, rev. ed. (New York: Continuum, 1996).

28. Roderick Ferguson, *The Reorder of Things: The University and Its Pedagogies of Minority Difference* (Minneapolis: University of Minnesota Press, 2012).

29. Sara Ahmed, *On Being Included: Racism and Diversity in Institutional Life* (Durham, NC: Duke University Press, 2012).

30. Carole Boyce-Davies, *Left of Karl Marx: The Political Life of Black Communist Claudia Jones* (Durham, NC: Duke University Press, 2007), 3, vii.

31. Rupan Bharanidaran, "Afrikan Student Union Releases Lists of Demands for UCLA Administration," *Daily Bruin*, May 11, 2017, https://daily bruin.com/2017/05/11/afrikan-student-union-releases-list-of-demands-for -ucla-administration.

32. W. E. B. Du Bois, *Black Reconstruction in America: Toward a History of the Part Which Black Folk Played in the Attempt to Reconstruct Democracy in America, 1860–1880* (1935; repr. London: Routledge, 2017).

33. A. O. Kawagley, *A Yupiaq Worldview: A Pathway to Ecology and Spirit* (Prospect Heights, IL: Waveland Press, 2006).

34. Somini Sengupta, "Protesting Climate Change, Young People Take to the Streets in a Global Strike, *New York Times*, September 19, 2019, https:// www.nytimes.com/2019/09/20/climate/global-climate-strike.html.

35. Robin D. G. Kelley, *Hammer and Hoe: Alabama Communists During the Great Depression* (Chapel Hill: University of North Carolina Press, 2015).

36. Movement for Black Lives, "Vision for Black Lives," M4BL, n.d., https://policy.m4bl.org/platform.

37. Movement for Black Lives, "End the War on Black People: All Relief Efforts Must Prioritize Black Families and Communities over Corporations," M4BL, n.d., https://m4bl.org/end-the-war-on-black-people.

38. Stanford Digital Repository, "Oral History Interviews with Local Blacks," n.d., accessed November 29, 2020, https://purl.stanford.edu/dt692 kf7259.

39. Student Nonviolent Coordinating Committee: Digital Gateway, "Photography Department," n.d., https://snccdigital.org/inside-sncc/sncc-national -office/photography.

40. Clarence G. Contee, "Du Bois, the NAACP, and the Pan-African Congress of 1919," *Journal of Negro History* 57, no. 1 (1972): 13–28; Carole Boyce-Davies, *Left of Karl Marx: The Political Life of Black Communist Claudia Jones* (Durham, NC: Duke University Press, 2007).

41. National Center for Education Statistics, "Enrollment," n.d., https:// nces.ed.gov/fastfacts/display.asp?id=98.

42. Bryan McKinley Jones Brayboy, "Hiding in the Ivy: American Indian Students and Visibility in Elite Educational Settings," *Harvard Educational Review* 74, no. 2 (2004): 125–52.

43. Vincent Schilling, "Mohawk Brothers Detained on Colorado Campus Tour Gain National Attention," *Indian Country Today*, May 10, 2018,

https://newsmaven.io/indiancountrytoday/news/mohawk-brothers-detained -on-colorado-campus-tour-gain-national-attention-s8rtk2HEWkaZHOGnim MFEQ.

44. E.A. Crunden, "University Apologizes to Native American Students Detained on College tour," *Think Progress*, May 5, 2018, https://thinkprogress .org/college-native-indigenous-students-police-892d58eaa65e.

45. Nikki Giovanni, *Chasing utopia: A hybrid* (New York: HarperCollins, 2013).

46. Vanessa Siddle Walker, *The Lost Education of Horace Tate: Uncovering the Hidden Heroes Who Fought for Justice in Schools* (New York: New Press, 2018).

CHAPTER TWO: SETTLER COLONIALISM

1. Scott A. Wolla, "The Rising Cost of College: Tuition, Financial Aid, and Price Discrimination," *Page One Economics*, 2014.

2. "Harvard University", Scholarships.com, n.d., https://www.scholarships .com/colleges/harvard-university.

3. McMullen, "For Many Black Millennials, Student Debt Is Biggest Hurdle in Homeownership."

4. Phone conversation with author, March 12, 2014.

5. Isis H. Settles, Nicole T. Buchanan, and Kristie Dotson. "Scrutinized but Not Recognized: (In)visibility and Hypervisibility Experiences of Faculty of Color," *Journal of Vocational Behavior* 113 (2019): 62–74.

6. Beverly Daniel Tatum, *"Why Are All the Black Kids Sitting Together in the Cafeteria?" And Other Conversations About Race* (New York: Basic Books, 2017).

7. Michele J. Eliason and Ruby Turalba, "Recognizing Oppression: College Students' Perceptions of Identity and Its Impact on Class Participation," *Review of Higher Education* 42, no. 3 (2019): 1257–81.

8. Nicole Watson, "The Land Is Our History: Indigeneity, Law, and the Settler State, by Miranda Johnson," book review, *English Historical Review* (2019).

9. Sharon Stein, "A Colonial History of the Higher Education Present: Rethinking Land-Grant Institutions Through Processes of Accumulation and Relations of Conquest," *Critical Studies in Education* (2017): 1–17.

10. Lorenzo Veracini, "Introducing: Settler Colonial Studies," *Settler Colonial Studies* 1, nod. 1 (2011): 1–12.

11. Christine E Sleeter, *The Academic and Social Value of Ethnic Studies: A Research Review*, (Washington, DC: National Education Association, 2011).

12. Bettina L. Love, *We Want to Do More Than Survive: Abolitionist Teaching and the Pursuit of Educational Freedom* (Boston: Beacon Press, 2019).

13. Jodi A. Byrd, *The Transit of Empire: Indigenous Critiques of Colonialism* (Minneapolis: University of Minnesota Press, 2011).

14. Patrick Wolfe, "Settler Colonialism and the Elimination of the Native," *Journal of Genocide Research* 8, no. 4 (2006): 387–409.

15. Kristine B. Patterson, and Thomas Runge. "Smallpox and the Native American," *American Journal of the Medical Sciences* 323, no. 4 (2002): 216–22.

16. Deborah Edwards-Anderson, "From Reconciliation to Resurgence: Dakota Commemorations of the US-Dakota War of 1862," *Middle West Review* 2, no. 2 (2016): 85–114.

17. Sylvia Wynter, "Unsettling the Coloniality of Being/Power/Truth/ Freedom: Towards the Human, After Man, Its Overrepresentation—an Argument," *CR: The New Centennial Review* 3, no. 3 (2003): 257–337.

18. Leilani Sabzalian, Rina Miyamoto-Sundahl, and Robin Fong, "The Time Is Now: Taking Initiative for Indigenous Studies in Elementary Curriculum," *Oregon Journal of the Social Studies* 7, no. 1 (2019): 6–19.

19. Claude M. Steele and Joshua Aronson, "Stereotype Threat and the Test Performance of Academically Successful African Americans," in *The Black–White Test Score Gap*, ed. C. Jencks and M. Phillips (Washington, DC: Brookings Institution Press, 1998), 401–27.

20. Ahmed, *On Being Included.*

21. antipodeonline, "Geographies of Racial Capitalism with Ruth Wilson Gilmore," June 1, 2020, YouTube video, 16:18, https://www.youtube.com /watch?v=2CS627aKrJI.

22. Patrick Wolfe, "Settler Colonialism and the Elimination of the Native," *Journal of Genocide Research* 8, no. 4 (2006): 387–409; Lorenzo Veracini, "The Imagined Geographies of Settler Colonialism," in *Making Settler Colonial Space: Perspectives on Race, Place and Identity*, ed. Tracey Banivanua Mar and Penelope Edmonds (London: Palgrave Macmillan, 2010), 179–97.

23. Roxanne Dunbar-Ortiz, *An Indigenous Peoples' History of the United States* (Boston: Beacon Press, 2014).

24. Stephanie L. Daza and Jeong-eun Rhee, "A Review of *Ecojustice Education: Toward Diverse, Democratic, and Sustainable Communities*," *Educational Studies* 49 (2013): 465–70.

25. Tressie McMillan Cottom, *Lower Ed: The Troubling Rise of For-Profit Colleges in the New Economy* (New York: New Press, 2017).

26. Wolfe, "Settler Colonialism and the Elimination of the Native."

27. Adrienne Green, "The Cost of Balancing Academia and Racism," *Atlantic*, January 21, 2016, https://www.theatlantic.com/education/archive/2016 /01/balancing-academia-racism/424887.

28. Hortense J. Spillers, "Mama's Baby, Papa's Maybe: An American Grammar Book," *diacritics* 17, no. 2 (1987): 65–81.

29. Mae Ngai, "Birthright Citizenship and the Alien Citizen," *Fordham Law Review* 75 (2006): 2521.

30. Cedric J. Robinson, *Black Marxism: The Making of the Black Radical Tradition* (Chapel Hill: University of North Carolina Press, 2000).

31. Craig Steven Wilder, *Ebony and Ivy: Race, Slavery, and the Troubled History of America's Universities* (New York: Bloomsbury, 2014).

32. Paolo Freire, *Pedagogy of the Oppressed* (New York: Continuum, 1970).

33. On plantation politics, see T. Elon Dancy, Kirsten T. Edwards, and James Earl Davis, "Historically White Universities and Plantation Politics: Anti-Blackness and Higher Education in the Black Lives Matter Era," *Urban*

Education 53, no. 2 (2018): 176–95. On the feminization of teaching, see Madeleine R. Grumet, *Bitter Milk: Women and Teaching* (Amherst: University of Massachusetts Press, 1988).

34. Ken Gonzales-Day, *Erased Lynchings Series*, 2006–17, James Park, CA, https://kengonzalesday.com/projects/erased-lynchings.

35. Carla Shalaby, *Troublemakers: Lessons in Freedom from Young Children at School* (New York: New Press, 2017).

36. Leigh Patel, "The Irrationality of Antiracist Empathy," *English Journal* (2016): 81–84.

37. Dunbar-Ortiz, *An Indigenous Peoples' History of the United States.*

38. Katherine I. E. Wheatle, "Neither Just Nor Equitable," *American Educational History Journal* 46, no. 2 (2019): 3.

39. Katherine I. E. Wheatle, "Neither Just Nor Equitable," *American Educational History Journal* 46, no. 2 (2019): 3.

40. US Congressional Record, 51st Cong., 1st Sess., June 14, 1890.

41. Donald A. Grinde, "Taking the Indian out of the Indian: US Policies of Ethnocide through Education," *Wicazo Sa Review* 19, no. 2 (2004): 25–32.

42. Wilder, *Ebony and Ivy*. "Cast on the underside of humanity" quoted from Wynter, "Unsettling the Coloniality of Being/Power/Truth/Freedom."

43. Stephanie Daza, Sharon Subreenduth, Jeong-eun Rhee, and Michelle Proctor, "Funding Re/De/Form in Higher Education: Diverse Points of Engagement," in *Neoliberalizing Educational Reform: America's Quest for Profitable Market-Colonies and the Undoing of Public Good*, ed. Keith Sturges (Leiden, Netherlands: Brill-Sense, 2015), 149–82.

44. Eve Tuck, "Suspending Damage: A Letter to Communities," *Harvard Educational Review* 79, no. 3 (2009): 409–28.

45. Leigh Patel, *Decolonizing Educational Research: From Ownership to Answerability* (New York: Routledge: 2015).

46. For "grit," see B. L. Love, "Black Women's Work: Resisting and Undoing Character Education and the 'Good' White Liberal Agenda," *Women and Migration: Responses in Art and History* 5 (2019): 17.

47. Eve Tuck and Monique Guishard, "Uncollapsing Ethics: Racialized Sciencism, Settler Coloniality, and an Ethical Framework of Decolonial Participatory Action Research," *Challenging Status Quo Retrenchment: New Directions in Critical Qualitative Research* (2013): 3–27.

48. M. A. Guishard, "Nepantla and Ubuntu Ethics para Nosotros: Beyond Scrupulous Adherence toward Threshold Perspectives of Participatory/Collaborative Research Ethics," PhD diss., Graduate Center, City University of New York, 2015.

49. James Baldwin, "A Talk to Teachers," *Child Development and Learning* (1963): 7–12.

CHAPTER THREE: PROFIT AND DEBT

1. Ahmed, *On Being Included.*

2. Stefano Harney and Fred Moten, *The Undercommons: Fugitive Planning and Black Study* (Wivenhoe, UK: Minor Compositions, 2013), 1.

3. Nick Estes, *Our History Is the Future: Standing Rock Versus the Dakota Access Pipeline, and the Long Tradition of Indigenous Resistance* (London: Verso, 2019), 6.

4. Tressie McMillan Cottom, *Lower Ed: The Troubling Rise of For-Profit Colleges in the New Economy* (New York: New Press, 2017).

5. William Beaver, "The Rise and Fall of For-Profit Education," American Association for University Professors, January–February 2017, https://www.aaup.org/article/rise-and-fall-profit-higher-education#.XemooDJKjjA.

6. Kevin K. Kumashiro, "Seeing the Bigger Picture: Troubling Movements to End Teacher Education, *Journal of Teacher Education* 61, no. 1–2 (2010): 56–65.

7. Andrew Rossi, "How American Universities Turned into Corporations," *Time*, May 22, 2014, https://time.com/108311/how-american-universities-are-ripping-off-your-education.

8. Cedric J. Robinson, *Black Marxism: The Making of the Black Radical Tradition* (Chapel Hill, NC: University of North Carolina Press, 2000).

9. Erica R. Meiners, "Ending the School-to-Prison Pipeline/Building Abolition Futures," *Urban Review* 43, no. 4 (2011): 547.

10. Cheryl Harris, "Whiteness as Property," *Harlem Law Review* 106, no. 8 (1993): 1707.

11. Jonathan S. Leonard, "Women and Affirmative Action," *Journal of Economic Perspectives* 3, no. 1 (1989): 61–75.

12. OiYan A. Poon, "Do Asian Americans Benefit from Race-Blind College Admissions Policies?," National Commission on Asian American and Pacific Islander Research in Education (2017), http://care.gseis.ucla.edu/wp-content/uploads/2015/08/care-brief-raceblind.pdf.

13. Benjamin Goggin, "Meet the Accused Ring-Leader of the Massive College Scandal, William 'Rick' Singer, the Owner of Edge College & Career Network," Insider.com, March 12, 2019, https://www.insider.com/william-rick-singer-the-accused-ringleader-college-admissions-scandal-2019-3.

14. Annie Lowery, "Her Only Crime Was Helping Her Kids," *Atlantic*, September 13, 2019, https://www.theatlantic.com/ideas/archive/2019/09/her-only-crime-was-helping-her-kid/597979/; Andrea Canning and Leezel Tanglao, "Ohio Mom Kelley Williams-Bolar Jailed for Sending Kids to Better School District," ABC News, January 25, 2011, https://abcnews.go.com/US/ohio-mom-jailed-sending-kids-school-district/story?id=12763654.

15. Craig Steven Wilder, *Ebony and Ivy: Race, Slavery, and the Troubled History of America's Universities* (New York: Bloomsbury, 2014), 11.

16. Joyce E. King, "2015 AERA Presidential Address Morally Engaged Research/ers Dismantling Epistemological Nihilation in the Age of Impunity," *Educational Researcher* 46, no. 5 (2017): 211–22.

17. Cherríe Moraga, and Gloria Anzaldúa, eds., *This Bridge Called My Back: Writings by Radical Women of Color* (New York: SUNY Press, 2015).

18. Linda Tuhiwai Smith, Eve Tuck, and K. Wayne Yang, eds., *Indigenous and Decolonizing Studies in Education: Mapping the Long View* (New York: Routledge, 2018), 14.

19. Gabriella Gutiérrez y Muhs, Yolanda Flores Niemann, Carmen G. González, and Angela P. Harris, *Presumed Incompetent: The Intersections of Race and Class for Women in Academia* (Boulder: University Press of Colorado, 2012).

20. Jens Peter Andersen, Mathias Wullum Nielsen, Nicole L. Simone, Resa E. Lewiss, and Reshma Jagsi, "Meta-Research: Is Covid-19 Amplifying the Authorship Gender Gap in the Medical Literature?," *arXiv preprint arXiv:2005.06303* (2020).

21. Dan C. Lortie, *Schoolteacher: A Sociological Study* (Chicago: University of Chicago Press, 2020).

22. Personal conversation with author, September 15, 2020.

23. Ahmed, *On Being Included.*

24. "Winners of the FY-2018 Competition Under the Defense University Research Instrumentation," US Department of Defense, 2018, pp. 1–6, https://media.defense.gov/2018/Apr/03/2001898629/-1/-1/1/FY18-DURIP-WINNERS.PDF?source=GovDelivery.

25. K. P. Griffler, *Front Line of Freedom: African Americans and the Forging of the Underground Railroad in the Ohio Valley* (Lexington: University Press of Kentucky, 2004).

26. Davarian Baldwin, "When Universities Swallow Cities," *Chronicle of Higher Education,* July 30, 2017, https://www.academia.edu/34268389/When_Universities_Swallow_Cities.

27. Stefan M. Bradley, *Harlem vs Columbia University: Black Student Power in the Late 1960s* (Urbana: University of Illinois Press, 2010).

28. University Statement on Empire State Development Corporation's Adoption of General Project Plan, Columbia University, July 17, 2008, https://manhattanville.columbia.edu/news/university-statement-empire-state-development-corporations-adoption-general-project-plan.

29. While We Are Still Here, *In the Face of What We Remember: Oral Histories of 409 and 555 Edgecombe Avenue,* 2008, Vimeo video, https://whileweare stillhere.org.

30. Gloria Ladson-Billings, "Toward a Theory of Culturally Relevant Pedagogy," *American Educational Research Journal* 32, no. 3 (1995): 465–91.

CHAPTER FOUR: FUGITIVE LEARNING IN SETTLER SOCIETY

1. Chinua Achebe, "The Truth of Fiction," *Hopes and Impediments: Selected Essays* (New York: Doubleday, 1989), 138–53.

2. Christopher Columbus, "Journal," *The American Yawp Reader,* n.d., https://www.americanyawp.com/reader/the-new-world/journal-of-christopher-columbus.

3. April Baker-Bell, *Linguistic Justice: Black Language, Literacy, Identity, and Pedagogy* (London: Routledge, 2020).

4. Leigh Patel, "The Ink of Citizenship," *Curriculum Inquiry* 47, no. 1 (2017): 62–68.

5. Gail Y. Okawa, *Remembering Our Grandfathers' Exile: US Imprisonment of Hawai'i's Japanese in World War II* (Honolulu: University of Hawaii Press, 2020), 123.

6. "Transcript: Read Michelle Obama's Full Speech from the 2016 DNC," *Washington Post*, https://www.washingtonpost.com/news/post-politics/wp/2016/07/26/transcript-read-michelle-obamas-full-speech-from-the-2016-dnc.

7. Roxanne Dunbar-Ortiz, *An Indigenous Peoples' History of the United States* (Boston: Beacon Press, 2014).

8. Joe Feagin, "Systemic Racism and 'Race' Categorization in US Medical Research and Practice," *American Journal of Bioethics* 17, no. 9 (2017): 54–56; Sylvia Wynter, "Unsettling the Coloniality of Being/Power/Truth/Freedom: Towards the Human, after Man, Its Overrepresentation—an Argument," *CR: The New Centennial Review* 3, no. 3 (2003): 257–337.

9. Dunbar-Ortiz, *An Indigenous Peoples' History of the United States*.

10. L. D. Wandner et al., "The Perception of Pain in Others: How Gender, Race, and Age Influence Pain Expectations," *Journal of Pain* 13, no. 3 (2012): 220–27.

11. J. D. Anderson and C. M. Span, "History of Education in the News: The Legacy of Slavery, Racism, and Contemporary Black Activism on Campus," *History of Education Quarterly* 56, no. 4 (2016): 646–56.

12. Nikole Hannah-Jones, interviewed by Trevor Noah, *The Daily Show*, February 5, 2020.

13. Christina Sharpe, *In the Wake: On Blackness and Being* (Durham, NC: Duke University Press, 2016).

14. Joel Spring, *Deculturalization and the Struggle for Equality: A Brief History of the Education of Dominated Cultures in the United States* (New York: Routledge, 2016).

15. *Black Panther*, dir. Ryan Coogler (2018; Burbank, CA: Walt Disney Studios Motion Pictures).

16. Vanessa Siddle Walker, *The Lost Education of Horace Tate: Uncovering the Hidden Heroes Who Fought for Justice in Schools* (New York: New Press, 2018), 140–41.

17. Walker, *The Lost Education of Horace Tate*.

18. MPD150, *How You Can Help*, June 2020, https://www.mpd150.com/how-can-you-help-mpls-june-2020.

19. Ruby Sales, interview with author, December 6, 2017.

20. Jarvis R. Givens, "Literate Slave, Fugitive Slave," In *The Future Is Black: Afropessimism, Fugitivity, and Radical Hope in Education*, ed. Carl A. Grant, Ashley N. Woodson, and Michael J. Dumas (New York: Routledge, 2020), 22.

21. Carter G. Woodson, *The Mis-education of the Negro* (1933; San Diego: Book Tree, 2006).

22. Leanne Betasamosake Simpson, *As We Have Always Done: Indigenous Freedom Through Radical Resistance* (Minneapolis: University of Minnesota Press, 2017).

23. Robin D. G. Kelley, *Freedom Dreams: The Black Radical Imagination* (Boston: Beacon Press, 2002).

24. Robin D. G. Kelley, "Black Study, Black Struggle," *Boston Review*, March 7, 2016.

25. Roderick A. Ferguson, *The Reorder of Things: The University and Its Pedagogies of Minority Difference* (Minneapolis: University of Minnesota Press, 2012).

26. Jay Gillen, *Educating for Insurgency: The Roles of Young People in Schools of Poverty* (Oakland, CA: AK Press, 2014), 27.

27. Rhea Estelle Lathan, "Testimony as a Sponsor of Literacy: Bernice Robinson and South Carolina Sea Island Citizenship Program's Literacy Activism," in *Literacy, Economy, and Power: Writing Research After Literacy in American Lives*, ed. John Duffy et al. (Carbondale: Southern Illinois University Press, 2013), 30–44.

28. United We Dream, "Toolkits & Resources," https://unitedwedream .org/tools/toolkits, accessed February 1, 2019.

29. Barbara Ransby, *Ella Baker and the Black Freedom Movement: A Radical Democratic Vision* (Chapel Hill: University of North Carolina Press, 2003).

30. C. J. Cohen, *Democracy Remixed: Black Youth and the Future of American Politics* (New York: Oxford University Press, 2010); United We Dream, "Toolkits & Resources."

31. Leigh Patel, "The SAT's New 'Adversity Score' Is a Poor Fix for a Problematic Test," *The Conversation*, May 22, 2019, https://theconversation.com /the-sats-new-adversity-score-is-a-poor-fix-for-a-problematic-test-117363.

32. Megan Bang, "Learning on the Move Toward Just, Sustainable, and Culturally Thriving Futures," *Cognition and Instruction* 38, no. 3 (2020): 434–44.

CHAPTER FIVE: THE STUDY TO STRUGGLE IS VULNERABLE

1. Ta-Nehisi Coates, *Black Panther: A Nation Under Our Feet, Book 2* (New York: Marvel Entertainment, 2017).

2. Stefano Harney and Fred Moten, *The Undercommons: Fugitive Planning and Black Study* (Wivenhoe, UK: Minor Compositions, 2013), 1.

3. Bettina L. Love, *We Want to Do More Than Survive: Abolitionist Teaching and the Pursuit of Educational Freedom* (Boston: Beacon Press, 2019).

4. "Seven Trends to Reform Teacher Education—Deans for Justice and Equity," National Education Policy Center, last modified October 10, 2019, https://nepc.colorado.edu/publication/seven-trends.

5. Harney and Moten, *The Undercommons*.

6. "FMFP History 101," Free Minds, Free People, last modified February 2019, https://soundcloud.com/free-minds-free-people/fmfp-history-101

7. Ahmed, *On Being Included*.

8. Roderick A. Ferguson, *The Reorder of Things: The University and Its Pedagogies of Minority Difference* (Minneapolis: University of Minnesota Press, 2012).

9. Ferguson, *The Reorder of Things*, 5.

10. Ferguson, *The Reorder of Things*, 3.

11. Ferguson. *The Reorder of Things*, 214.

12. Crystal Marie Fleming, *How to Be Less Stupid About Race: On Racism, White Supremacy, and the Racial Divide* (Boston: Beacon Press, 2018).

13. US Department of Education, National Center for Education Statistics, *The Condition of Education 2019 (NCES 2019–144), Characteristics of*

Postsecondary Faculty, https://nces.ed.gov/fastfacts/display.asp?id=61, accessed December 20, 2019.

14. Ahmed, *On Being Included.*

15. Liliana M. Garces and OiYan Poon, "Asian Americans and Race-Conscious Admissions: Understanding the Conservative Opposition's Strategy of Misinformation," University of California, Los Angeles, Civil Rights Project/Proyecto Derechos Civiles, 2018.

16. Matthew Johnson, "Managing Racial Inclusion: The Origins and Early Implementation of Affirmative Action Admissions at the University of Michigan," *Journal of Policy History* 29, no. 3 (2017): 462–89.

17. Subini Ancy Annamma, Darrell D. Jackson, and Deb Morrison, "Conceptualizing Color-Evasiveness: Using Dis/ability Critical Race Theory to Expand a Color-Blind Racial Ideology in Education and Society," *Race Ethnicity and Education* 20, no. 2 (2017): 147–62.

18. Garces and Poon, "Asian Americans and Race-Conscious Admissions."

19. Ellen Berrey, *The Enigma of Diversity: The Language of Race and the Limits of Racial Justice* (Chicago: University of Chicago Press, 2015).

20. Savannah Shange, *Progressive Dystopia: Multiracial Coalition and the Carceral State* (Durham, NC: Duke University Press, 2017), 10.

21. Ida Bae Wells (@nhannahjones), December 16, 2019, https://twitter.com/nhannahjones/status/1206681718054432768.

22. Ruby Sales, interview with author, December 6, 2017.

23. Sales, interview with author, December 6, 2017.

24. Personal communication with author, December 10, 2017.

25. "US: Brown University Votes to Divest from Business Violating Palestinian Rights," *MEMO: Middle East Monitor*, December 3, 2019.

26. Scott Jaschik, "U Chicago to Freshmen: Don't Expect Safe Spaces," *Inside Higher Ed*, August 25, 2016, https://www.insidehighered.com/news/2016/08/25/u-chicago-warns-incoming-students-not-expect-safe-spaces-or-trigger-warnings.

27. Dorothy E. Roberts, *Killing the Black Body: Race, Reproduction, and the Meaning of Liberty* (New York: Vintage Books, 1999).

28. Nirmala Erevelles, "In Search of the Disabled Subject," in *Embodied Rhetorics: Disability in Language and Culture*, ed. James C. Wilson and Cynthia Lewiecki-Wilson (Carbondale: Southern Illinois University Press, 2001), 92–111.

CHAPTER SIX: STUDY AND STRUGGLE

1. Harney and Moten, *The Undercommons*, 63.

2. Christina Pazanese, "Giving Du Bois His Due," *Harvard Gazette*, October 24, 2018, https://news.harvard.edu/gazette/story/2018/10/harvard-sociology-conference-to-give-web-du-bois-his-due.

3. Alleen Brown, "Indigenous Women Have Been Disappearing for Generations. Politicians Are Just Starting to Notice," *The Intercept*, May 31, 2018, https://theintercept.com/2018/05/31/missing-and-murdered-indigenous-women.

4. Human Rights Campaign, "Fatal Violence Against the Transgender and Gender Non-Conforming Community in 2020," n.d., https://www.hrc.org /resources/violence-against-the-trans-and-gender-non-conforming-community -in-2020.

5. John Carlos and Dave Zirin, *The John Carlos Story: The Sports Moment That Changed the World* (Chicago: Haymarket Books, 2011).

6. "Women's History Month: Rosa Parks," *Reproductive Health Access Project* (blog), March 18, 2018, https://www.reproductiveaccess.org/2018/03/womens -history-month-rosa-parks.

7. See chapter 4's discussion of the Morrill Acts.

8. Mark Sandritter, "A Timeline of Colin Kaepernick's National Anthem Protest and the Athletes Who Joined Him," *SB Nation*, September 25, 2017, https://www.sbnation.com/2016/9/11/12869726/colin-kaepernick-national -anthem-protest-seahawks-brandon-marshall-nfl.

9. Kristine B. Patterson and Thomas Runge, "Smallpox and the Native American," *American Journal of the Medical Sciences* 323, no. 4 (2002): 216–22.

10. la paperson, *A Third University Is Possible* (Minneapolis: University of Minnesota Press, 2017).

11. Ashon Crawley, "Otherwise, Ferguson," *InterFictions Online: A Journal of Interstitial Arts* 4 (November 2014).

12. Vanessa Siddle Walker, *The Lost Education of Horace Tate: Uncovering the Hidden Heroes Who Fought for Justice in Schools* (New York: New Press, 2018).

13. Colleen Flaherty, "Making Diversity Happen," *Inside Higher Ed*, September 28, 2017, https://www.insidehighered.com/news/2017/09/28/how-two -institutions-diversified-their-faculties-without-spending-big-or-setting.

14. William Edward Burghardt Du Bois, *The Philadelphia Negro* (1899; New York: Cosimo, 2007).

15. Gloria Anzaldúa, *Light in the Dark, Luz en el Oscuro: Rewriting Identity, Spirituality and Reality* (Durham, NC: Duke University Press, 2015), 134

16. Eve Tuck and K. Wayne Yang, "Decolonization Is Not a Metaphor," *Decolonization: Indigeneity, Education & Society* 1, no. 1 (2012): 1–40.

17. Eve Tuck, "Suspending Damage: A Letter to Communities," *Harvard Educational Review* 79, no. 3 (2009): 409–28.

18. Sylvia Wynter, "Unsettling the Coloniality of Being/Power/Truth/ Freedom: Towards the Human, After Man, Its Overrepresentation—an Argument," *CR: The New Centennial Review* 3, no. 3 (2003): 257–337.

19. Walidah Imarisha, Robin D. G. Kelley, and Jonathan Horstmann, "Black Art Matters: A Roundtable on the Black Radical Imagination," *Red Wedge*, July 26, 2016, http://www.redwedgemagazine.com/online-issue/black -art-matters-roundtable-black-radical-imaginatio.

INDEX